After-School Drama for Kids

by Shauna Ray Ratapu

©2014 by Shauna Ray Ratapu

The moral rights of the author have been asserted

This book is copyright. Except for the purposes of fair reviewing no part of this publication may be reproduced or transmitted in any form or by any means, electronic or mechanical, including photocopying, recording or any information and retrieval system, without permission in writing from the author/publisher.

For my children: Nathan, Starr and Noel.

And for my ever-patient, ever-supportive husband and

love of my life, Phillip.

I love you once, I love you twice, I love you more than beans and rice.

Table of Contents

Introduction: You Don't Need Experience! (Or, Fake It Till You Make It!)   6

Step 1: I Dreamed a Dream! Imagine your Ideal Drama Program   12

Step 2: WHO will be coming to your drama group?   14
    Inclusivity, Culture and Children with special needs   15

Step 3: WHAT will you be doing or working towards?   17

Step 4: WHEN will you hold your classes/meetings?   19

Step 5: WHERE will your classes/meetings be held?   21
    Things to consider when searching for a suitable Drama space: 21

Step 6: The Big HOW?   30
    The rules or "The business meeting"   30
    The Structure – how the time in class is used   32

Step 7: Some Dramatic Points about Drama OR "The Stuff"   35
    Voice: The first job of an actor is not just to be heard, it is to be understood!   35
    Body: Show don't tell   37
    Movement: Even in stillness, there is movement…of time   38
    Space: The final frontier OR It's all about the Space…   39

Step 8: Putting the PARTY in Policy and Procedure   43
    Outline of Policy and Procedure Manual   45

Step 9: Plan of Attack OR The Zen of Lesson Planning   48
    Planning for multiple abilities   50
    A Possible Future You: Help! I've used up my first 10 lessons!   52

Step 10: Let's Do This! The Final Checklist!   53

Bonus Chapter: The BIG Show!   55

Your First 10 Lessons   68
    Lesson 1   68
    Lesson 2   70
    Lesson 3   72

Lesson 4	*74*
Lesson 5	*76*
Lesson 6	*78*
Lesson 7	*80*
Lesson 8	*82*
Lesson 9	*84*
Lesson 10	*86*
The Stuff	**87**
Warm ups	*88*
Games	*103*
Exercises	*113*
Index	**120**

Introduction: You Don't Need Experience! (Or, Fake It Till You Make It!)

I have always been the kind of kid who loved to tell big whopper stories, most of which would be so convincing that I'd actually start to believe them myself. I even thought I could tap dance when I never had a lesson. I was the neighborhood 'director', getting as many willing participants as I could to act, watch, and conduct the many backstage activities in our garage/black box theatre.

My parents weren't the type to see the value in all of my theatrical endeavors, but saw fit to label me the family "drama queen," which I would have worn with pride had it not been used as a dismissive insult. Honestly, I was a bit of that drama queen; without the resource of the stage and acting out stories to occupy my ever-expanding imagination, I, unfortunately, took my drama off stage and into real life.

Obviously I survived, but I always knew that my pre-teen and teenage years would have been so much more enjoyable if I had theatrical Drama as an outlet. I tried getting into Drama at school but I had already decided that I wasn't good enough, or confident enough to be onstage with all the outgoing, popular kids. Instead, I withdrew and became increasingly detached from school, friends and family. Growing into an adult, I felt like I had no real direction. I couldn't decide what I wanted to do – well, I always knew what I wanted to do, but what I needed to do felt like a different story. I wanted to perform! I had always wanted to perform. I knew that if ever given the chance, I'd be great at it. It wasn't just about the performance for me, it was about the story – how it was told and how the audience responded. But what I needed to do was feed myself. I didn't come from a wealthy family and I had been on my own before I even finished high school. To me, and to most of the "adults" I knew, acting and Drama as a career was impractical. So, I got busy trying to earn a living and kept my imagination and passion for the stage in check.

In hindsight, I believe that I actually had it all backwards. I needed to explore Drama as an outlet. I needed to immerse myself in stories; it was how I made sense of my own life story. Of course I needed to eat and have a roof over my head, but there was no reason I couldn't pursue a career somewhere within the realm of the Dramatic Arts. In fact, when I was 18 I got a job at a movie theater and it was one of the greatest years of my life for making friends and being what we called "Theater Geeks". We weren't acting or performing but we were certainly soaking up as many movies as we could and imagining ourselves as actors, directors, producers, costume designers, cinematographers, and all the rest. We needed storytelling in our lives.

This belief is what inevitably led me to starting my own after-school drama workshops and my own black-box theatre company, but my three children were my real inspiration. I wanted my children to know that they could always pursue their dreams and to never give up on them just because some people don't think they were "practical". So, I set the example – if I could do it, so could they.

When my oldest child was nine, he suddenly began to show signs of depression. He was an exceptionally bright kid, but I felt that he wasn't being challenged enough at school and my husband and I were at a loss to keep up with his insatiable thirst for information. Then, one day while driving through Olympia, Washington, I saw a sign that said *Capital Playhouse* and remembered a radio ad I'd recently heard which advertised a summer kids' theater program. My gut told me to stop, and the kids and I went in to see what it was all about.

Playhouse was offering four-week summer holiday programs which would end in a full-scale production of a popular musical, starring all kids under 16. The price just about knocked me off my seat ($500 per kid!), but they took payments and said it could be paid off over the whole year, which was a deal-sealer for us!

I signed my oldest up for the musical *Once on This Island* and my middle child up for the "Tots" program which was designed for kids aged three to seven. Those four weeks were life-changing for our whole family. We saw something emerge from our two older kids that we'd always suspected was there, but could have never imagined would make them this happy.

The next three summers were filled with musical theater bliss. Our kids thrived in the mixed-age environments and we made life-long friends. Capital Playhouse was also a semi-professional theater company in the other nine months of the year and, after seeing how happy my kids were, I decided to try my luck and audition. To my utter surprise (and horror!), I was cast as a tribe member in the musical Hair! (It was only after being cast that I was told I'd have to bare all for the famous nude scene...but that's another story, for another book!)

In October 2002, our family relocated to a small town on the east coast of New Zealand. There were a couple of community theater groups, one of which was offering an after-school drama club, but it wasn't as structured as we would have liked and I was afraid my kids wouldn't be as challenged as they were with Capital Playhouse. Knowing how much they were missing having Drama in their lives (versus the capital D drama of our chaotic new lives) I devised a plan to start my own After-School Drama business!

Gisborne, New Zealand, my husband Phillip's home town and where we have lived for the past 12 years, is a city of about 40,000 people, many of whom live rurally. It is also quite isolated, the closest city of its size is three hours away. This meant that opportunities to be exposed to different kinds of arts were limited. When Phillip was in high school here he was introduced to Modern Dance by his Drama teacher and was also involved in his school plays (Grease and Jesus Christ Superstar) which, at that point had seemed to have gone down in Gisborne history as the greatest performances of all time by a local high school. The high school dance troupe he belonged to had become famous throughout New Zealand and Australia and they were able to take their shows to America. From there, Phillip was granted a scholarship to the University of Utah, and nearly 20 years later, he returned home with his American wife (me!) and three kids. Drama gave him the opportunity to have a much needed creative outlet which he excelled in and was able to take all over this world. I recognized that while there were a lot of local sports opportunities for kids in Gisborne, there was hardly anything in the way of creative arts outside of what was offered in school and that there were a lot of talented kids around, just like Phillip, who were just waiting for an opportunity to creatively express themselves!

Shooting Starz Creative Drama Workshops was born a few months after moving to New Zealand and my kids and their new friends loved it! I had no experience other than the three years as a "theatre mom" to my kids, my own short stint in a semi-professional production, plus a class or two at the local community college, but this felt like a calling!

I enlisted the help of a new-found friend of my own, hired a space from a local community theater group, and started to advertise. Before I knew it, my classes were filling up and we were having a blast! I advertised Shooting Starz as "creative drama workshops" rather than "theater for kids" or "Drama" because I wanted to send the message to parents that this was a creative endeavor rather than a set-in-stone script type thing, and the word "workshop" was used to put emphasis on the working part or the creative process rather than the end result. In fact, I never intended to have an end-of-term or end-of-year show. This was suggested to me by the kids and the parents, all of whom expressed their desire to show what they'd been working on. For me this should have been obvious, but I was trying so hard to live in the creative moment that I overlooked the fact that Drama is realized in the sharing of the story or the performance, and it was only in that moment that it all made sense.

After two years running Shooting Starz, I felt the need to complete my education and become fully qualified as a teacher. Thus, I ended my business and began to study full-time. Four years later, I was a fully-qualified High School Drama Teacher. I wanted to teach high school drama rather than elementary school drama because my children were getting older and I wanted to follow their progress and interests. I also wanted a regular pay check! Running the workshops was never about the money, but it did need to pay for itself and a little extra was even better. But I have to emphasize the "little" part - it was never going to make us rich – except in spirit and adventure!

I taught high school drama for three years and found it to be too rigid and confining for both my liking and the students' as well. They always loved the warm up games and improvisation lessons but when it came down to the requirements of theory and practice set out by the curriculum, I felt there was a huge portion of creative freedom and expression being lost on all but the highest of achievers. My passion was still with the young people who were like I was in school – not the most confident or the best singers, but the ones who really had a story to tell. So, when my son left home for university, I suddenly got the pang to go back to my original plan: After-School Drama.

At the end of 2011, I left my full-time teaching job and opened *Unhinged Productions* – an after-school and school-vacation drama program for kids aged 7-16. The name Unhinged came out of my need to be free again, and I liked the connotation that you were a little bit crazy if you were "off your hinges". I was a little bit crazy to do what I did – with absolutely no capital to invest, I rented a space and with Phillip's help, turned into what I'd always dreamed of, a black-box theater and a place of wonder, imagination and fun!

At the end of the two years, I was unable to continue as my youngest child has a disease called Spinal Muscular Atrophy Type 3. Her mobility had deteriorated to the point where I now had to be home full-time. With my older two children grown and off to university, and my youngest having an interest in Art and Photography rather than Drama, I was happy to return to being home full-time, helping my husband with his business and thinking about my next creative adventure.

My time with Shooting Starz and Unhinged was filled with so much joy and laughter as well as many awkward, unpredictable moments, not to mention real-life struggles (financial, cultural, and emotional), I feel it would be a waste not to share them with others who are looking to begin a similar journey. It is with this thought in mind that I share my experiences and at the same time wish you all the joy, laughter and success...with as few awkward and painful moments as I have seen.

That said, this book is about taking what I've learned through experience over the past 15 years and turning it into an easy, 10-step process to get started, 10 1-hour lessons (that's 10 weeks if you're doing one per week!) and true stories of DELIGHT and DISASTER to make you laugh, think, prepare and plan for ultimate success and fun. I also include a large list of games, ice breakers and other ideas to keep your programs fun and exciting. As the crème-de-la-crème, I will give you a step-by-step guide to putting on The Big Show, the end of semester production guaranteed to get the kids and families to come back year after year!

Step 1: I Dreamed a Dream! Imagine your Ideal Drama Program

My idea of the perfect After-School Drama program was, at first, a bit naïve. I wanted it to be about the process rather than the product, which is something I still believe in very much. I've seen too many kids' shows where everyone is so stressed out about getting it perfect for the final curtain, and to me, it just never seemed like fun – oh sure maybe for the overachievers, but for everyone else, it was a major chore or a major bore.

I wanted my classes to be about the creative process, not about getting to the end result. So we worked on an end-of-year performance for family and friends, but that performance didn't necessarily need to be perfect. Boy was I wrong! AND boy was I right! At the end of my first year, with my first production, I learned that half the parents and students were super happy with everything even if it wasn't perfect, and the other half were highly embarrassed and frustrated at the lack of attention to detail.

In order to appease both sides I decided to make the classes into beginning and advanced, both with mixed ages but that came with its own problems of exclusivity, parents thinking their children should be in the advanced class when clearly they did not, and so on. So back to the drawing board I went.

First I thought, what did I want? More specifically, what did I want for my children? I decided that this should be my compass point and that it was pointless to do something that fell outside of what I truly believed in, otherwise I would surely fail at it.

Another very important thing to think about is: What do you want for you? Yes, you are important too! What amount of time and energy are you willing to put into this, because if you don't make a solid plan in the beginning, it can very easily get away from you. Energy is especially important to pay attention to. Drama kids require lots and lots of positive, lively energy to bounce off of. Your mood and tone set the mood and tone of the class. Herein lies the true test of my mantra: Fake It Till You Make It!

I can't tell you the amount of times I felt like a sack of wet napkins right before a class, but I had to muster the energy to go in and treat those kids and that class like it was the best part of my day and their day! If it's just an hour and you've had a down day, those kids have no idea and do not deserve to know how bad your day has been...it's not their problem, so keep it all in and Fake It Till You Make It...then go home and have a glass of wine and talk about the funny stuff that happened in class. I guarantee that your hour with Drama kids will be the best therapy you never paid for!

Speaking of paying, do you want to get paid or will this be a purely volunteer venture? Shooting Starz and Unhinged were both structured as businesses while the other group in town was mainly a volunteer type of club, with very minimal club fees. I based my fees on what other extra-curricular activities were going on in town for kids and decided on $10 per lesson, or $100 per 10-week semester/term. If the term was a little short or long here in New Zealand, I kept it at a clean $100. I also allowed families to pay weekly or in increments if that made it easier - returning the favor that we had when we were with Capital Playhouse was important to me.

Unhinged Productions 2013

STEP 2: WHO WILL BE COMING TO YOUR DRAMA GROUP?

I guess you could say that Step 1 dealt with the "Why?" question in that you would have asked yourself, "Why am I wanting to do this?" So, naturally Steps 2-5 are about the other four W's: **Who** are the kids who will be coming to your Drama group? **What** will you be doing when they get there? **When** will your group meet and Where will your meetings/classes be held?

When I first started *Shooting Starz* I had four age groups: 3-5, 6-9, 10-13 and 14+. In theory this should have worked nicely, but in practice it was always a big mess. The reason is that some kids who were mature 5's, 9's and 13's were more suited for the classes above and some older kids were definitely more at home with the younger ones. The 14+ age group was always a hard one to keep going because in our small town there just were never enough high school aged kids who were committed to coming week after week.

In addition, I needed to teach to all four different levels of understanding, interest and attention span (for instance, three-year-olds can hold it together for about two minutes at a time!). This became a problem time *and* energy-wise and after the first 10-week school term I scrapped the 3-5 year olds, as an hour was too long for them anyway. I then ran only two different groups: 6-10 and 11-14+, which worked great because it basically separated the elementary school kids from the middle school and high school kids.

When I started *Unhinged* a few years later, I was able to 'hit the stage running' so to speak because I knew that I would really only need to run two different types of classes: Primary (Elementary) and Intermediate (Middle School). I did also run one high school class because there were a few kids who wanted more of a challenge, but in the end I cancelled it due to the small number of students vs my time involved.

INCLUSIVITY, CULTURE AND CHILDREN WITH SPECIAL NEEDS

You must consider that when you are working with kids, not all of them are going to be the same. Well, thank goodness for that! Wouldn't the world be a boring place if we were all carbon copies of each other? It seems like a no-brainer, but I have had quite a few hard lessons in cultural sensitivity that I feel the need to pass on.

When I started *Shooting Starz*, I was brand-new to New Zealand. Although New Zealand is an English speaking country, it is also a Te Reo Māori speaking country and the other official language is Sign. While being very familiar with the English language, I was not familiar with the other two, even though my husband is Māori. I was also not familiar with New Zealand culture, Māori culture, or deaf and disability culture…yet. I made a lot of assumptions that I shouldn't have and found my way through by making an incredible amount of embarrassing and sometimes hurtful mistakes. Sometimes parents were nice about it and sometimes they weren't.

***Delight: Language 101.** I once had two students, a brother and sister, whose first language was Te Reo Māori. They spoke English but they went to a Māori school and were, at that point, only fluent in reading and writing in their own language. We were doing some script work and although I had considered that some of my younger students would need extra help with the reading, I hadn't really considered it for my older students (this was a mixed-age group). By now I had lived in New Zealand for almost 10 years and I had special training in Māori culture as well as a Post Graduate degree in Cross-cultural communication but somehow I still found myself in unchartered territory – mostly because I had made an* *assumption and so was caught without a plan of inclusion.*

I wanted these two students to feel totally included and to be able to participate in the way they felt most comfortable. So, I spoke to their mother about it and together we decided that we could translate the play into Te Reo Māori and that they could do their parts in their language. They were happy with that at first, but later decided that they wanted to say their parts in English. Their mother was totally happy either way and in the end it was their choice, they did what they felt would make them most comfortable. The fact that they returned for another school-vacation program told me that they felt included and enjoyed it and so did their family!

In the future classes, I always made sure to be prepared for not only children who may read, write or speak another language, but also for children who were dyslexic or had other learning difficulties. Children come with all sorts of physical differences too. I mentioned in my introduction that my youngest child is in a wheelchair. She wasn't always wheelchair bound but she was always very unsteady on her feet. When she was much younger and would attend my classes, we would always make sure that she could keep up with our games, or make sure that she could still participate while sitting. I never wanted her to feel that she had to sit something out just because it was too physical – there's always a way to improvise and adapt to someone's ability. **Drama is using your imagination so who says you have to play by the exact rules of anything!** Navigating is easier if you have contingency plans and aren't afraid to improvise!

Step 3: What will you be doing or working towards?

When my kids were at *Capital Playhouse* the format (in my mind) was simple: Rehearse a musical for four hours per day, five days per week for four weeks. At the end of it they performed a professional-quality musical production complete with costumes, set, music and everything else that goes with it. It was a major undertaking and we were never disappointed in the caliber of performance or appearance. The $500 per summer was definitely put to good use.

For my two Drama programs however, I purposely chose a different route in order to focus more on the process of Drama rather than the final performance as well as to keep costs down. So, instead, I focused on the basics of Drama: **Voice Projection, Story-telling, Movement, Improvisation, Imagination and Role-Playing.** We created little scenes, played a lot of Drama games and practiced silly walks, accents and characters. At the end of the 10-week term we would put on a little show for family and friends that reflected what the kids had been learning. I wanted the parents to see that their kids were having fun first and that through the fun, they were actually learning life-long skills. The first half hour of class would usually be Drama games and skill building and the second half hour would be dedicated to rehearsing for our show, which was usually a 15-minuted scripted fairy tale. Eventually however, I moved away from using scripts for the younger group as they tended to focus way too much on either knowing or not knowing their lines rather than getting involved in the story. I will talk more about this in The Big Show!

Delight: After a frustrating time trying to get the kids to remember to bring their scripts to class, my assistant Ashley and I decided to come up with our own play idea and see if the kids could just improvise their parts. We decided to pretend to get trapped inside an imaginary box...you know, like the ones mimes are famous for making. We told the kids that it was their job to come up with creative ways to get us out. The ideas were so unexpected and wonderful! They ranged from detonating a nuclear explosion, to simply "un-imagining the box"! Each of the 10 students came up with a unique way to get us out and for each example, the rest of the students were to help.

One gorgeous girl who always did things slightly differently than everyone else surprised us all by cutting an imaginary hole in the imaginary box, hopped in with us and then showed us the way out. It was so simple and cute, and she so honestly believed that we were trapped in there that I just wanted to relive that magical moment again and again. Sadly, when it came time to recreate the moment for friends and family on our show night, it just didn't happen – but lots of other unpredictable and magical moments did happen and the families were delighted with their children's creativity and sense of adventure!

Step 4: When will you hold your classes/meetings?

Term 3 2013

We are now an OSCAR approved programme, so families who qualify may apply for WINZ subsidies for children ages 5-13.

Term 3 Workshops start 29 July and run through the school term.

In addition to skill building, drama games and theatresports, each class will be working towards a short performance at the end of the term; so students enrolled in two days will get to perform in two pieces!

Cost is $75 + GST Per term ($86.25). (Students must stay with the days they have enrolled in and cannot interchange due to class number restrictions)

*discount available for families with more than one child enrolled

Classes are limited to 10 students so enrol now to ensure a spot!

Mon	Tues	Weds	Thurs	Fri
(Primary)	(Intermediate)	(Primary)	(Intermediate)	(Primary)
3:30-4:30	3:30-4:30	3:30-4:30	3:30-4:30	3:30-4:30
4:30-5:30	4:30-5:30	4:30-5:30	4:30-5:30	4:30-5:30

The title of this book might be "After-School Drama for Kids" but it doesn't have to mean literally after the school day. You can hold Drama classes on the weekends, in school holidays or yes, after-school. I chose to offer classes in the following format during the school term.

I never managed to fill the 4:30 to 5:30 slots but I usually had enough overflow from the 3:30 to 4:30 classes to keep them open. You might have noticed that the price listed on this schedule is different than the $100 per term that I mentioned earlier. This is because I became an official "After-school" program and was eligible for funding, which enabled me to pass some savings along to students' families.

If you are just organizing one after-school or school-vacation group, you might want to make it more than an hour for one or two days per week. When I held school-vacation programs, they were always two hours long, with a short break in the middle for using the restroom and having a light snack. However, two hours is way too long, in my opinion, for after-school programs as the kids have already had a long day at school and some will be struggling to focus and energize for games, while others will still be bouncing off the walls!

Finally, be warned that at the end of a school term, kids can really lose momentum. This is to be expected, especially towards the end of the school year. For Drama teachers however, this can be frustrating if you are trying to put together an end-of-term or end-of-year show. You'll have to rely on the belief that once the kids get up on that stage, they'll suddenly be charged with a million volts and will delight their audience who will give them nothing less than a standing ovation at the end…or not, but hey, **Fake It Till You Make It!**

Step 5: WHERE will your classes/meetings be held?

When I started *Shooting Starz*, I approached a local community theater group and asked if I could rent their rehearsal space. They were very obliging and offered it to me at a $100 per 10-week term. The only problem for me was that I couldn't make the space my own and when the group were rehearsing for a play, it made it very difficult for me to keep students from interfering with their sets and costumes.

I dreamed of having my own theater space that I could turn into a place of magic and wonder for all ages. *Capital Playhouse* felt like that for our family and so it was a long time goal for me to open my own theater space. When I decided to leave my teaching job and open *Unhinged*, I really only ever considered one space – we transformed it into everything I'd always dreamed of. Oh it had its problems though: high rent, freezing in winter and boiling hot in summer, very grumpy neighbor who liked to poison us with his toxic fumes and other little annoyances. But for all its faults, it was really a magical place!

Things to consider when searching for a suitable Drama space:

Space – you need enough space in a space! To decide on whether a space is too big or too small, try to imagine how many kids you'll be working with at one time all in a circle with their arms spread out wide, finger tips touching. If you just imagine them huddled on a mat, it won't give you an idea of how much play space you'll actually need. This is another reason to ideally keep the numbers lower rather than higher (10-12 is ideal).

You also need to consider room for parents who might want to stay and watch, as well as other siblings.

A space can also be too big. If a space is too big, like a school or church hall, it can easily be modified by using a large mat or carpet remnant to define the "play space". Failing that, you can use tape to mark off an area, which will help the kids feel the boundary and not to "get lost in space".

How do *you* loo? (Restrooms) – This is actually a huge consideration. Your space will need accessible, safe toileting areas. Safe as in, they are in the room you are using or in a supervised space adjacent. You can't be sending kids off to the restrooms by themselves unless the restroom is in the room itself. If you are teaching by yourself, and there are no parents who can monitor a child needing to use the restroom, what would you do if you had a kid who suddenly needed to "go" and the only restrooms were down a hall in an empty part of a building? You'd have to take the whole group with you that's what...kids can't always hold it until break time, so this is a biggie. You will also need a wheelchair accessible restroom.

***Disaster**: I made the big mistake of putting one of those gel air fresheners in the restroom at my Unhinged space. It smelled really nice in the bathroom, but not so nice when it was smeared all over one of my seven-year-old student who thought it smelled nice too!*

***Moral**: Safety first! Keep anything that you don't want little hands to find well out of reach!*

Let there be SOME light! – The good thing about Drama is that you don't need to have a space with a lot of windows or mirrors - just enough lighting to see and to be safe in. *Unhinged* was literally a black box with no windows, although it did have clear light panels in the roof. This was great until the sun beat through them and roasted us all – and no windows meant no ventilation, so in the summertime we had to keep the doors open, which made it noisy from the street traffic.

Cold floors and hot seats – *Unhinged's* floor was painted concrete, which I loved for staging productions and painting sets. But it was a bit hard for the kids and very cold in the winter. I invested a couple hundred dollars in a large rug which we used as our meeting mat and it was great for starting and ending the classes.

I had a few chairs and old couches around to use when doing skits but also for parents to sit in when they watched. I found that you can never have too many stackable chairs!

To stage or not to stage! A "stage" can just be a designated area, it does not have to be elevated, and in fact, with kids it's sometimes better if it isn't because they fall off...ALL-THE-TIME! If you do have a stage, be sure that's it is only one step high and is well distinguishable from the floor around it, in other words, not the same color. I had a black stage and a black floor which I finally had to trim in bright white just so that people would stop falling off! I fell off once but made it look so stylish that everyone thought it was part of what I was demonstrating! AGAIN, **Fake It Till You Make It!**

Fire and Ice! I've mentioned it a few times, but dealing with temperatures is a huge consideration when working with kids. If it's too cold or too hot you're going to run into more than a few problems with behavior, focus and energy, not to mention parents don't want to sit in a stuffy or freezing space while waiting for their kids to finish their activities. Safety is obviously a factor here as well.

Shooting Starz was held in an old converted church and so it was huge and hard to heat in the winter. They had installed gas heaters which did an okay job but only just took the edge off in the dead of winter. They were also smelly, and I've never been a fan of gas heating. *Unhinged* had a large stand-alone firebox in the main space. When lit, it would warm up the mat area but nothing else and sometimes we would spend the whole hour right in front of it because it was too cold to move anywhere else. Not ideal.

Delight: Once I staged a play in the middle of winter at Unhinged. We had a full house and the ambiance with the fire going was amazing. It was still VERY cold, so fortunately I had a large amount of fur coats in my costume collection for just such an occasion and the audience members were so pleased when we handed these out plus whatever blankets we could muster for extra warmth.

Safe and Sane: It seems like a no-brainer but any space where children are going to be running around in, should be 100% safe and free of hazards. If an area within the space is off limits, be sure to mark it or secure it. At *Unhinged* we had a moveable staircase that went up to a loft area that was used for storage. It was totally off-limits to the kids and we made sure to put signs and ropes up to remind them. They were of course mesmerized by the thought of what could be lurking up there – whether it be monsters or treasure - and because their imaginations were so amazing, they were always tempted to have a look, so at the end of every term I would let each child go to the top of the stairs, peek into the dark abyss of the loft and then come down – SLOWLY.

Disaster: Our Unhinged building shared a wall with an auto repair shop. Our first day of class was about to start and one of the kids and her mom showed up about 20-minutes early. As I was showing them around the space, there came a sudden toxic mist that engulfed the whole building. The smell was so volatile we were all gagging and ran outside to see what it was and where it had come from. The neighbor was spray painting a car radiator outside rather than in a designated spray booth and the fumes were all going straight into my studio! I was horrified and so was this poor mom who was about to leave her child in a toxic space. I told her I would sort it out and that if the fumes didn't clear out that we would cancel the classes. This would have been absolute financial ruin for me on the first day as most of the families had already paid in advance and most of the money had already been spent on the rent and renovations!

I marched over to the auto repair shop and begged them not to spray paint any more until we found a solution to stop the fumes from coming into our building – and that's when the neighbor wars began! Thankfully, the guy who was doing the actual spraying was just a worker there and he happened to have a heart AND a conscience and told me he wouldn't spray during my classes anymore and if I gave him the times, he'd work around it.

The first class was saved, but there were many classes over the two years that had to be cancelled or that were accosted mid-class with toxic fumes because there were other people spraying besides the nice guy who tried to keep from poisoning us. I would always take the kids outside or to the front of the studio when this happened, but it interrupted the flow, and made the kids sick. The parents and I complained to the City Council and I begged the landlord to sort it out, but in the end, it was always just a hit and miss.

Moral: Before you sign a lease, make EXTRA sure that the building is 100% safe to work and have kids in. This could have been the end of a business before it even got started and was surely a pain in my side for two years!

Unhinged Studio before "Black Out"

Unhinged Studio after "Black Out" Floor still not done.

Painting the Set

Our first Set for our first end of term show at Unhinged

Unhinged in full swing!

High School group performing at Unhinged

Step 6: The Big HOW?

So how's this all going to work? You know what you want, why you want it, who is coming, when and where it will be, but how in heck are you going to pull this off? Well, that's a good question (and probably the trickiest!) By now you can probably guess what my answer to that would be...that's right! **FAKE IT TIL YOU MAKE IT!**

Now I'm not suggesting that you completely wing it – that would be like an actor going on stage in front of an audience without reading a script or even knowing what the play's about. I am suggesting however, that once you're prepared and have a fair idea of the direction you want to go in, then you just do it and let it all unfold, figuring out how to navigate as best as you can. The key is to be prepared and organized and to be FLEXIBLE! (More on that in Step 9)

Most teachers have a way of relating to kids that works for them. Of course, if you've never worked with kids or have limited experience other than your own children or your nieces and nephews, then you'll need to develop your style as you go along. With Drama, it's all so about co-creating, that is: give and take between you and the kids. Co-creation is very different than say, coaching a sports team, where the rules of the game are the rules of the game and the main goal is usually to win. In Drama, there are no hard and fast rules, but you can co-create a few with your students in order to make everyone's experience more enjoyable. So, you might develop a style and strategy completely different to mine, but for now I will pass on what, through much trial and error, has worked for me.

The rules or "The business meeting"
When I first started teaching after-school Drama I read a book called *Kids Take the Stage* by Lenka Peterson and Dan O'Connor. It was my bible for the first year and I highly recommend it in addition to this one! One of the most valuable suggestions for me from that book was the concept of the

"business meeting". This was where the first meeting or class of every term and with every new group, would have the first 15-30 minutes dedicated to the "business meeting". Each of the class participants imagined that they were very important board members of a business...this business was...you guessed it! SHOW BUSINESS! And that each member would help to decide HOW it was all going to work.

Discussion points, for my classes, were always around three main things:

RESPECT

SAFETY

And

FUN!!!

The RESPECT part involved discussions around not talking over each other or the teacher, no put downs, being supportive and encouraging each other. Respect was also for the space, the things in it and so on. The Business Partners would all have a chance to chime in and then, it would be decided that the Value of RESPECT would always be honored.

The SAFETY part involved obviously physical safety – no hitting, no running, jumping over chairs or going into off-limits zones, but also, and very importantly with Drama kids, *emotional safety*. Many parents put their children into Drama to help them overcome shyness and to build confidence. Therefore, maintaining the idea of **building children up** rather than **tearing them down** is one of the main goals; keeping an emotionally safe environment is of the utmost importance! I use examples with the students like "How would you feel if you were on stage doing your best, and someone from the audience yelled out, 'Haha, he's dumb! What a dork!'" The kids usually laugh nervously because this might not have even occurred to some of them. While you might be putting a bit of fear into them, they should all think about how that would feel if it happened to *them* so they don't make the mistake of doing it to *others*.

Once they've decided what it means exactly to be respectful and to be safe in the Drama classroom, they should then help to decide on the **consequences** if someone goes against these co-constructed values. For this, I usually like to have a bit of fun...because as you may have noticed, we haven't gotten to the FUN part yet, but we're about to. I ask the kids, "What should we do if someone says something unkind to someone else, or laughs at them or calls them a name? Should we hang them from the rafters or should we make them eat a whole bag of brussel sprouts?" This shows the kids that I have a sense of humor but also that THEY can probably come up with something better. It usually dissolves into some ridiculous punishments before we get to some real consequences, and these are always gently led to appropriate, non-humiliating ones that I've already decided on. One consequence is to just apologize, and another, if it happens more than once, is to sit out until they feel that they can honor the values that they participated in co-creating. I always remind them that they were at the "business meeting" and that everyone agreed that the values needed to be upheld in order for everyone to have FUN!

Finally, the FUN part, I explain to them, can only happen when *everyone* is enjoying themselves, including the teacher – and that the only way for that to happen is for *everyone* to stick to the values of RESPECT and SAFETY (including the teacher).

THE STRUCTURE – HOW THE TIME IN CLASS IS USED

I must digress a bit here and say that before the "business meeting" on the first class of each new term or group, there should always be INTRODUCTIONS. All of my classes started in the same way: Everyone sitting in a circle on the mat. I'd usually ring a bell or make a funny noise to let them know that class was starting and to come join the circle. If it is the first class and if there are new kids, it is to be expected that some will hang back or want mom or dad to sit with them. I never pushed kids to join in if they were feeling shy. Usually just seeing the other kids laughing and having fun was enough to get them to warm up and join in.

Introductions are important for breaking the ice and for you, as the teacher, to see just who is shy and needs some prompting, and who is very boisterous and might need some guidance on how to share the stage. Each person says their name, nice and loud so we can all hear it, and then says one thing they like and one thing they dislike. For elementary aged kids, I leave it at that, but for the middle school kids, I turn it into a memory game where I go first and then the next person says, "Her name is Shauna and she likes Drama but does not like pickles. My name is Jeff and I like soccer but I do not like my little sister." The next person in the circle has to remember, my name and likes/dislikes, then Jeff's, and then add his or her own. Round it goes and the poor kid at the end has to memorize the whole lot. I try to not have them do more than 5-7 at a time unless they really want to. IMPORTANT: if a person doesn't want to participate they can always say "pass" and it should be no big deal. They'll come around when they start to feel more comfortable and trusting.

Okay, so INTRODUCTIONS are just for the first day of the first class, but if you are holding weekly classes, the kids might forget each other's names in the meantime so there are other ice breaker games you can play in the first 5-10 minutes so that they can familiarize themselves again. These games are listed in the index under "Ice Breakers: Name Games".

Here's how I typically structured my classes:

Circle time (5-10 minutes): I would talk about what we were doing that day and ask if anyone had anything exciting to share that they could share in 30 seconds or less.

Warm ups (5-10 minutes): Fun warm up games to get the kids in the Drama zone, laughing and having fun.

Games (10-15 minutes): A game is usually a warm up game with a bit more substance

Lesson (10 minutes): Focusing on a particular aspect or skill of Drama, I would spend about 10 minutes teaching this – however, I have found that demonstrating these lessons is far more fun and interesting than me droning on about them for 10 minutes. Learning is in the doing – and if I could demonstrate this whole book to you, I certainly would!

Exercise to "stick" the lesson (10 minutes): I've listed several exercises in the index that will help the kids to practice their new skill.

Games (5-10 minutes): A fun game to end with is always a great way to ensure that the kids have a "Fun Sandwich" – Fun on the ends and learning in the middle. Of course, it should all be learning and all be fun and they really shouldn't notice the difference between the bread and the filling!

Circle time - Wind down (5 minutes): I always tried to regroup the kids for the last five minutes in order to settle them and to talk about what we'll be doing next time. This would also be a time to remind them of any upcoming notices.

If you are rehearsing for an end-of-term or end-of-year show, then simply skip out the lesson, exercise and final game and replace with show practice.

STEP 7: SOME DRAMATIC POINTS ABOUT DRAMA OR "*THE STUFF*"

So, it should be easy enough to read about how the games, warm-ups and exercises are played, but I thought I would add some points on Drama techniques (The Stuff) so you can start to build your classes around them. This is also pretty cool for the parents. When they ask their kids what they learned in Drama today, the kids can say, "We learned about PROJECTION!" Rather than, "Nothing, we just played some games." *Bang for buck* is what they say here in New Zealand – meaning *Get your money's worth*.

For Elementary aged kids, I focus on these four aspects of Drama:

Voice

Body

Movement

Space

My next book will explore these in more detail and will also delve into Middle and High School Drama, but for now I will give basic points about what each one means in Drama and how to build lessons around them. If you are already familiar with Drama skills and techniques, feel free to skip this chapter!

VOICE: THE FIRST JOB OF AN ACTOR IS NOT JUST TO *BE HEARD*, IT IS TO *BE UNDERSTOOD*!

The word 'projection' is used a lot in Drama. Without proper guidance, kids can easily mistake PROJECTING their voice with YELLING. I tell them that there is a difference between the audience hearing them and actually understanding what they are saying on stage. Projecting your voice is a technique that comes with practice and it is about using your diaphragm rather than just your vocal chords. The first of the ten lessons I've included in this book contains a fun 'projection' lesson and accompanying exercise.

Along with projection, which is the most basic of Voice techniques, there are these elements to keep in mind:

Pitch: The highness or lowness of voice – i.e. when someone's really excited or nervous, the pitch of their voice can be high and squeaky.

Tone: I tell the kids it's not *what* you say, but *how* you say it that changes the tone. To demonstrate I use the example of a Mom calling out to one of the kids, "Tommy, come here please" can be said in different tones which would tell Tommy different things. If it sounds like he's in big trouble, he may not want to "come here" so quickly.

Volume: This is different to projection in that even if a character is 'whispering' to another character on stage, the volume is down but they still need to project their voice in order to be heard and understood.

Pace: Beginning actors tend to say their lines too quickly. How fast or slow we speak carries meaning. I usually go back to a Mom or Dad speaking to their children because the kids always find it funny. If I say the same thing, such as "Have you done your chores?" using a different pace, it will carry a different meaning and the kids can see this right away when it slooowwwwssss down.

Pause: I love teaching kids the importance of the 'pause'…

See what I did there? You were expecting something weren't you? I call that a 'pregnant pause'. It gives the audience a sense that something really big or important is about to be revealed. Pauses, when used wisely, can add DRAMA, SUSPENSE, INTRIGUE and EXCITEMENT into a story more than any other technique! They can also cause the audience to think that an actor has forgotten a line, so they have to be used deliberately and with body language to emphasize the point the actor is making.

I didn't include **Accent** because that's just too much information for littlies to take in. It doesn't mean that if someone brings it up you can't talk about it but one of the dangerous things about going into accents with younger students is often times they immediately go to a stereotypical accent of a particular culture or ethnicity – someone of that ethnicity might be in the class and it can all turn very uncomfortable for you as the teacher, the student who is being stereotyped and the parents watching. So, my best suggestion is to say to the kids: When you imitate the way someone speaks or moves, make sure you are doing your best to sound and move just like them and not an exaggeration of them, otherwise it's just poking fun and not acting.

BODY: SHOW DON'T TELL

Young actors tend to disconnect their body if they're focused on using their voice to demonstrate a character and vice versa. The point of teaching them about the different ways of using Voice, Body, Movement and Space in Drama is to eventually help them to integrate them all together in order to bring their characters and stories to life. One of my mantras is "Acting without using your WHOLE body is like playing the piano with just one finger". It would have made an even bigger impact on the kids if I'd actually had a piano to play (or knew how, which I don't) but the message was usually pretty well understood.

There are lots and lots of warm ups, games and exercises that help the kids to tune into using their whole bodies while acting. It's important for Drama kids to become conscious of body language and how it's just as effective at telling someone what you want or how you feel as actually saying it with your voice – and actually, it's probably MORE effective. This is where I usually go into the idea of "Show, don't tell", by "showing" them rather than "telling" them how powerful body language can be.

Here are some elements to focus on when teaching about Body techniques in Drama:

Posture: The stance or way of holding your body.

Gesture: The movement of any part of the body to express idea, feeling or mood. I have had some great times doing little scenes where the kids can only use their eyebrows to "talk" to one another.

Body awareness: The ability to select appropriate use of body on stage, choosing to use the whole body, or isolated parts of the body expressively.

Facial expression: Using the face to show mood, emotion, feeling and responses

Eye contact: Establishing eye contact with another actor or the audience. Again, there are quite a few fun games which help to establish the use of eye contact. As kids get older, eye contact between actors becomes harder because it suggests an intimacy or a knowing of what's going on behind the eyes. The sooner kids get comfortable with doing this in Drama, the better their performances will be, but also it helps so much with connecting to characters, each other, other characters in the scene and the scene itself.

MOVEMENT: EVEN IN STILLNESS, THERE IS MOVEMENT...OF TIME

The concept of movement in Drama involves EVERYTHING that moves physically in a scene as well as everything that is in a scene moving through time. For instance, a group of kids create a scene about a group of time travelers who are looking for a long lost map that will lead them to a great treasure. The map, whether it's represented or not in the scene, presumably moves through time even if it never physically moves. The way the characters move their bodies to show that they are speeding up as they go into the future or slow down as they come back to the present, are all important in effectively telling the story to the audience.

Here are some basic points about Movement:

Timing: How fast or slow you move and how long you move for.

Direction: Where you are going: forwards, backwards, diagonal, sideways, up or down.

Energy: The amount of energy used in movement can show a character's mood, urgency or age.

Group Movement: At the more advanced level this is also known as *Ensemble Awareness*. It is moving as part of a group, proximity to other actors, responding to other actors' movement. The game 'Follow the Leader' can be played in many different ways and is a great way to demonstrate Group Movement.

Pathways: The pattern of movement you create in the space, e.g. curved, straight or zig-zag pathways. Again, using the game 'Follow the Leader', you can demonstrate different Pathways while also paying attention to Group Movement, Energy AND Timing. Kids love playing this game, especially because they each get turns at being the Leader.

Repetition: Repeating a movement or recycling a movement for emphasis.
Repetition: Repeating a movement or recycling a movement for emphasis. ;-)

SPACE: THE FINAL FRONTIER OR IT'S ALL ABOUT THE SPACE...

I've said it before and I'll say it again (Ha! Repetition!): You need enough space in a space...in order to define it, move in it, shape it, shrink it, grow it, show it – know it! Remember the little story about how my assistant Ashley and I did a play with our students about us being stuck inside an imaginary box? Well that whole term we were working on the concept of Space with the students. We didn't tell them what we were going to do before we did it, because we wanted to see what their reactions would be. First we did a bit of mime discussion and demonstration. We had everyone do a miming warm-up and game. Then Ashley and I got onto our little stage and asked if they thought that Ashley and I would be able to mime building an imaginary box together. So they all sat on the mat and became our audience as we attempted to build an imaginary box.

The first problem arose when we went to build the top of the box (this was planned), because Ashley is quite a bit taller than I am, so I was having to jump up to help her build the roof and the kids thought this was hilarious. Then, I insisted that we build a floor to the box and Ashley said (again, planned but somewhat improvised) "But we're standing on a floor. Why do we need to build one?" To which I replied, "Uh, Duh Ashley! We're standing on a REAL floor and we're trying to build and IMAGINARY one! We need to build the floor!" Being so tall, Ashley acted like it was a great chore to get down on the ground to build the imaginary floor of the box and the kids roared with laughter. What we had just demonstrated to them was the concept of LEVELS within Space.

Once the box was complete, Ashley and I pretended we couldn't get out and then had a pretend argument about whose job it was supposed to be to build the door. We pretended that we could no longer see the kids but that we could hear them and it was so funny to see their reactions while pretending not to see them. Of course they did what came naturally – they all ran straight up and into the imaginary box to show us how silly we were for thinking it was real. This gave us the opportunity to have them join in the scene and to also pretend that Ashley and I were stuck in the box and that they were now free to do all the things they'd always wanted to in Drama but were not allowed! Without careful discussion and reiteration that this was just pretend and that we were all acting, it could have gotten way out of control and, at times, it did – mainly because the kids became so good at defining the Space, that they started to believe that Ashley and I were really trapped and therefore wouldn't be able to stop them from, say, going UP THE STAIRS to the OFF LIMITS LOFT! So, we built that into the play as well.

Here are some elements of Space:

Levels: low, medium, high. Ashley and I demonstrated this by using our height differences in a funny way.

Personal space: your own space, the bubble immediately around your body, how you use this space. While Ashley and I were trapped inside the imaginary box, I pretended to get very claustrophobic while Ashley pretended to stretch-out and use as much space as she liked, disregarding respect for my personal space and making me feel even more crowded and trapped. The kids got such a kick out of this…and we did too, being the clowns we are.

General space: all other space in the room, how you use this space. Architecture the physical structures of the space you are in and within the space, how you use and interact with these structures. When we began practicing this piece, it was chaotic because the kids wanted to run around and just be crazy in all the spaces that were outside the imaginary box. We had to stress to them that there would eventually be an audience there, and they needed to pretend that the audience was there even when they weren't in order to get a sense of where to go and what to do so that the audience could still see them. As mentioned, the stairs and loft area were always off limits and the kids had sort of created their own mythology about what might be up there. So we allowed ONE student to go half way up the stairs while another student got to scream in the most dramatic way "STOP!!!!! DON'T GO UP THE STAIRS!", which then had the whole audience turning around in their seats to see who was trying to head up the stairs and what might happen next. Needless to say, the student was stopped by the faint sounds of Ashley and my voices – well we were really loud but the kids pretended that they could just barely hear us…oh it was fun. So much fun.

Proximity: The amount of distance or space between actors, the amount of space between actors and audience. In a black box theater like Unhinged, everything happens up close and personal. This can either be a great thing for an audience, or a very intimidating thing. Some audiences love the anonymity of being able to sit in a darkened theater and 'just watch', knowing the actors are practically blinded by stage lighting and so can't really see who is or isn't out there. Other times, audiences feel privileged to be close to the stage and the actors. Sometimes the actors include the audience in a bit of interactive theater. It all depends on what you want the audience to feel, see, hear and do.

There is so much more I could delve into about teaching Drama, but I said this was an easy 10-step guide, not a post graduate thesis, so I won't go into any more than those basics in this book. As I mentioned, my next book will have more Drama content, while this one just focuses on getting the program up and running. Please don't think you have to be an expert in the field of Drama before starting a group with kids – you remember what it was like to pretend, just go with that and you'll do great OR **Fake It, Till You Make It!**

STEP 8: PUTTING THE PARTY IN POLICY AND PROCEDURE

Even though the words 'Policy and Procedure' threaten to put you to sleep or to throw this book out the window (but probably not if you're reading via Kindle!), I am going to make a valiant attempt to put the PARTY into P & P!

The first thing you should know is that while seemingly tedious, P & P is one of the most necessary steps of starting up a Drama group/business/club for kids. In fact, it is crucial for the smooth running of classes, dealing with parents' questions and concerns as well as taking quick, decisive action in emergencies – minor or major.

You might be saying to yourself, "Oh come on, this isn't rocket science, let's just get on with it!" and believe me, I said the same thing. That is, UNTIL the questions/concerns started coming in and I had no answer – this is where **Fake It Till You Make It** can only take you so far. When dealing with the safety and well-being of other people's children, you had better have a solid answer to a worried parent's question.

Okay, so like I said, it doesn't have to be a yawn fest. I suggest you throw a PARTY! Yes, a P & P PARTY! Get a few of your closest friends together and make a fun night out of brainstorming your Policies and Procedures. Have fun with it! Go wild! Seriously, think of the most ridiculous things that could happen and see what your friends come up with. Be sure to write them down. This is Drama we're talking about remember, not an Accounting Club...anything goes!

Delight: *After our group 'Business meeting' we would always go on a 'safety tour' of the studio. Usually I would have a returning student lead this tour and they always got great pleasure out of doing it. First we would come to the 'emergency exit' which would lead into a discussion about why we might possibly need to use the emergency exit.*

One of my students who lead this tour several times loved to tell the class of how the time elephants fell from the sky and so we all had to get into a single file line, trying not to get squashed, and then, we had to walk, not run, to our designated meeting spot. Sadly, we realized (too late) that if elephants were falling from the sky, that there was nothing we could really do about it to keep safe. Being outside where we could look up and dodge them was probably the safest thing we could do.

Of course we did go into the real procedure as well, but this was all made much more fun by us trying to stay in a single file line, not running, until we got to the big open grass lawn that was the 'designated safety area' where I let the kids run around dodging falling elephants.

I suggest having a Policy and Procedure Manual which you can build over time. Here I have listed some things you will need to consider and these can be topics of exaggerated (and serious) discussion at your P & P PARTY!

Outline of Policy and Procedure Manual

Mission Statement: What are your classes about?

Service Environment: What are the things that parents and children should expect when kids are attending your classes? Think about: STANDARDS, GUIDANCE, ACTIVITIES, SAFE PREMISES, TOILETS, PHONE SERVICES

Service Operation: What sort of day to day or class to class responsibilities will you put in place regarding attendance and enrolment? Think about: ENROLMENT PRACTICES (i.e. forms with contact information, things you should know about your students like allergies, injuries, learning or behavioral difficulties), ATTENDANCE PROCEDURE, COLLECTION OF CHILDREN (i.e. Who is or IS NOT permitted to pick children up?), TRANSPORTING CHILDREN (i.e. in case you go on a field trip), COMPLAINTS PROCEDURE (thankfully I never had to use this, but I had a procedure and a form, just in case), BEHAVIOR MANAGEMENT, RESPONDING TO CULTURAL ISSUES, CHILDREN WITH SPECIAL NEEDS OR DISABILITIES, RECORD KEEPING.

Health and Safety: How will you ensure that your students are kept safe both emotionally as well as physically? Think about: RISK ASSESMENT (i.e. What could go wrong with an exercise or activity? Falling off the stage was usually my biggest worry), ACCIDENTS & INCIDENTS (you should always keep records of accidents as well as 'near misses'), UNWELL CHILDREN (What do you do when kids come to class feeling unwell or become unwell during class – I've had a few vomit moments – not fun, but at least I had a plan), EMERGENCIES (like elephants falling from the sky, or earthquakes, fire...toxic fumes).

Staff Behavior: You may not decide to hire helpers, but even if people - including parents - are volunteering to help, they should still uphold a Code of Behavior and sign it. Think about: EXPECTATIONS FOR COMMUNICATION, DUTY OF CARE, AWARENESS OF P & P, MAINTAINING PROFESSIONAL BOUNDARIES. In addition, I always had my staff or volunteers go through a vetting procedure, whereby they were cleared by the Police Authority which did a background check. This was NOT standard procedure when we first came to New Zealand and we were quite shocked at the relaxed attitude in regards to adults working with children. It has since changed and is now a requirement thankfully, so be sure to check with your local authorities as to what your specific requirements might be.

Supervision: This includes adult to child ratios and knowing where the students are at all times.

Disaster: The Hider. I once had a very terrifying Drama Teacher Moment (DTM) when one of my students thought it would be funny to hide from the class. This happened right before it was time to go home so of course parents were coming to collect their kids, and the whole class was frantically searching for The Hider! There were plenty of places to hide because I had racks of costumes lining all but one of the walls, she could have gone upstairs to the off-limits loft – or worse, she could have left the premises!!

I was nearly in tears, and the rest of the students were all very concerned. Parents coming in to pick up their kids joined in the search while I prayed that we find The Hider before her parents came in. Then, just as I was about to go into full-blown panic mode, someone called out "Found her!" and we all ran to the direction of the voice. Turns out that the little 'darling' was hiding behind the bathroom door. We had checked the bathroom several times but we didn't expect that she would be in there and not answering us. Her mother turned up just as we found her and a few of the parents that were searching told the mom before I even had a chance – I was thankful for that because I was so angry that I probably wouldn't have handled it very well.

The Hider's mother scolded her very harshly in front of me and what was left of the class. Turns out she was hiding because she loved Drama so much that she didn't want to go home. This softened my heart a bit, until I remembered that this was Drama class, and I was teaching these kids to be little actors. I might have believed her if it hadn't happened again...

To sum up, you do not have to have all of your policy and procedure done and dusted 100% before you start (unless your city ordinances dictate that you do of course). However, it would be good to have a few loose ideas written in draft form that you can finalize as you go. I would also highly recommend having Enrolment sheets, Attendance sheets and Class Flyers with Times and Dates pre-printed and ready to go. These can always be amended as needed.

Step 9: Plan of Attack or The Zen of Lesson Planning

There are two approaches to planning and implementing lessons. Well, I'm sure there are way more than two approaches, but I feel that they may all fall into either of these two categories which I call 'Attack Mode' or 'Zen Mode'. Both have their place and each mode is suited to different circumstances.

For basic day-to-day Drama teaching, I use 'Zen Mode'. This is a planned, but FLEXIBLE approach that tends to follow the mood and flow of the class. For instance, I may have certain lessons, exercises and games planned for an Elementary class on Tuesday, but it turns out to be a very hot day and the things I had planned just seem like way too much effort and exertion for the kids. So, I quickly switch gears and get the kids into imagining they are ice skating, swimming, making snow people, and other things that will take them out of the feeling of being so hot. We might do less physical stuff and more introspective stuff, or we might even do an art project.

Another example of the 'Zen Mode' is when a class takes an unexpected turn or students stumble upon an idea that you would like to see them expand on. I always have a plethora of games, exercises and scene ideas both in my head and at my fingertips in my trusty Drama Handbook – which is something I've developed over the past 12 years (stay tuned as this is my next book project), which I can pull from if we need to go in a different direction than what I planned.

'Attack Mode' is saved for working towards The Big Show. Sometimes kids don't want to rehearse and I have made the mistake of thinking that making them rehearse is cruel and so I've switched back into 'Zen Mode' when I should have gone full steam ahead. The best way to ensure that this is well understood is to put it in writing so the parents know what's going to happen, and to remind the students that at a certain point in the term, they will be having one half of the class time dedicated to rehearsals until it gets closer to performance time and then the whole class will be dedicated to rehearsals. I call this 'Attack Mode', because there is no easy way to put on a show – well, there is, but it usually ends up in DISASTER!

Disaster: One term, I decided to not push the students into learning their lines for our short end-of-term play. I told the parents that they should leave their scripts with me – and this was because I was tired of so many kids forgetting to bring them to class. A few of the really determined kids insisted upon taking their scripts home, but these were the ones who always brought them back AND knew all their lines, so I wasn't concerned. On the performance night, I'd never had so many students on stage holding their scripts in front of them. It was the slowest, and most painful performance in the history of performances – I felt bad for everyone who had to sit through it, but especially for the students who'd worked hard to learn their lines and their parents.

At the end of the night, I emphasized that the important thing was that they were up on stage in front of an audience. That was only partly true and I knew it, but at the time I didn't know what to do about it. I wanted to teach kids who were at all levels and not just the high achievers so I was at a loss about what to do to make it fun, rewarding and challenging for everyone. That's when I decided to raise my expectations. When I raised my expectations and relayed what they were to the kids and their parents, the next end-of-term performance was a million times more enjoyable for kids, their families and for me!

Planning for multiple abilities

Okay, so how *do* you plan for multiple abilities? In Drama, it usually tends to naturally move in the directions the kids want it to. The ones who love the stage tend to try to expand their new skills into Oscar winning performances and the ones who are shy or struggling, are able to look towards the others as role models and as examples of how to (or how not to) do something. I'm also always on hand to help them get through. When it comes to script reading, I choose an age-appropriate, fun script and say that if anyone needs help reading that it's okay, I'll help or someone else can help with that. For non-readers, I say their lines first and then they repeat, adding their own personality. As mentioned earlier, I usually use scripts only as guidelines for Elementary kids. I want them to get inside the story and learn to improvise rather than to rely on what a script says line-by-line.

IMPORTANT: The only other thing I can say about teaching to multiple abilities is that you won't know how to teach the child until you know the child. You must become the student and learn how different children tick before you can best serve their needs.

*Delight: **Purple Princess**. I taught a gorgeous girl who I shall call Purple Princess. Purple Princess was quite high on the autistic spectrum. She was really set on doing her own thing but at times wanted to participate as long as it was on her terms. As long as she wasn't a danger to herself* *or others, I allowed her to do her thing. However, I would always ask if she wanted to join in and would never move on to the next thing without trying to include her. Eventually, she joined in more and more. My assistant Ashley and I were just as encouraging and generous with our praise for her as we were with anyone else and so were the other students. They all understood that she marched to the beat of her own drum and were okay with it.*

After attending classes with us for a year I began to see an amazing thing happen with Purple Princess. She would actually initiate ideas and was engaging at high level although would occasionally break off and do her own thing. I realized that when she did this, it was because to her something wasn't right and the only way she could communicate it was to break away from the group. I would then go to her, while Ashley worked with the group, and together, Purple Princess and I would come to a solution to the problem. Sometimes it was that she wanted a different costume, or she didn't want to be a certain character anymore. Another time it was because another student was bullying her quietly and neither Ashley nor I caught it. As I observed her behavior over the two years, I really began to understand how best to serve her. Watching Purple Princess onstage was such a delight and always pleasantly surprising because of her unique way of seeing the world.

A Possible Future You: Help! I've used up my first 10 lessons!

Don't panic. Even if you haven't got a handle on writing your own lessons, if you've done all 10 lessons in this book, then it must mean you've gotten through 10 classes and that's HUGE! Surely you know which of the games, lessons, warm ups and exercises the kids really responded to and which ones maybe didn't go so well. Make notes after every class to remind yourself of what worked and what didn't and the possible reasons why or why not.

Before I start each term I always set a goal or a direction I would like to head in (One term the goal was to get students to improvise an entire story). Then, I do a rough outline of what I'd like to cover in each lesson. After that, I just flesh it all out. Remember that FLEXIBILITY is key and that you can change course anytime you want if things seem to be leaning in a different direction. Also, always be sure to have more tricks up your sleeve than you think you'll need.

Finally, a word about timing. Sometimes you and your students can be so wrapped up in a scene or a fun moment that the time gets away on you and before you know it, class is over. This happened to me SO MANY TIMES! It's not so great for parents if they have to wait around, especially if they have other children in tow or someplace else to be. For me, I sometimes had classes that immediately followed and so it was a bit more hectic than I would have liked. I finally got in the habit of setting my phone alarm to go off 5 minutes before the end of class in order for me to get the group settled on the mat again and to recap the session or to give out reminders.

STEP 10: LET'S DO THIS! THE FINAL CHECKLIST!

If you are able to check off everything in this list, then you are ready to roll!

- ☐ You have checked with your city/state/country rules and regulations and have complied with all necessary requirements for working with children.

- ☐ Your classes are going to be held in a safe, comfortable environment with clean, adequate and accessible restrooms.

- ☐ You have a very clear idea of what to do in case of emergencies and have established an emergency exit procedure.

- ☐ You have a first aid kit.

- ☐ You have enrolment forms which when filled out, will be handy in case you need to call a child's parent.

- ☐ You have attendance sheets ready so that when the kids show up their parents can sign them in and out.

- ☐ You have a schedule of times and dates.

- ☐ You have read this book!

Okay, if you've checked everything off, then you must be ready to advertise and get some students! There are so many things I could have added to this list, but I didn't want to bog you down. You will know where there are gaps. The best way to prepare yourself is to visualize the first class from beginning to end. See yourself in the space waiting for your class to arrive and imagine how they will come in, what you will say to them and to their parents, what they might need, ask, do. Then walk yourself through the class. Is there anything you need? A bell, a mat, some objects or bits of costume that you can keep in a plastic box or small trunk? Is there anything the kids need? Access to drinking water? Band-Aids? Ice packs? Finally, visualize the end of the class. How will you finish off your first class? What will you say to the kids and the parents? What will they say? Will you ensure that they leave with approved people and sign out? Will you make sure they have all their stuff (e.g. backpacks, jackets, shoes)? Will you make sure you don't have A HIDER and that all the kids have been collected before you lock up and go home? Yes? Okay! GO GET EM TIGER!

AND...ACTION!

Bonus Chapter: The BIG Show!

Putting on a show can be as exciting as it is scary! I have directed everything from large-scale musical productions for high school, to professional theater, to very low-key "show-'em whatcha got" nights for kids and the one thing they all had in common was the fear-factor, i.e. Will the audience like it? Will something go wrong? What if so-and-so forgets their cue? What if it rains?! That's never going to go away so don't let it stop you from trying. That said, there are a few things you can do in order to help make your production go smoothly (although Murphy's Law takes precedence, be ready for it), and for you, as organizer or director as well as for everyone else involved to enjoy the process not just the end result!

1) First and foremost, prior to doing anything else – even before deciding on what you'll be performing – **assess your resources.**
   - How are you placed for help? **Never** try to put on a show alone. There are always parents who are chomping at the bit to be asked to help, so ask!
   - What is your budget going to allow for regarding script royalties, costume, stage, lighting, sound, and advertising? For instance, if you have a budget of $500 for a show, you're probably not going to be able to put on a full-scale production of *Les Miserable*…unless of course you have A LOT of donations of people's time, money, skills and energy.
   - What do you have on hand that you can put to use? I had a costume hire store, so I always had a huge array of costumes to choose from. I also have graphic design skills, so I designed my own ads, flyers, tickets and posters. Start tapping your own and others' skills and resources – you might find that someone has a surplus of pirate costumes in their basement which could lead to you deciding to do *The Pirates of Penzance*!
   - Where will you be performing and how big is the stage? Some shows require a lot more acting space than others.
   - How big is the audience area and do you have enough chairs? If you have 10 students, then plan on each student bringing four

people. Most students will only bring two, but others will bring their entire extended family – better safe than sorry.
2) **Choose the play or performance sequence you will do.** You may need to pay royalty fees; this is standard practice if you are using a published script. Remember, someone relies on income from those royalties, so although it may be tempting to just photocopy a script and perform it, most theater practitioners will find that to be in very poor form. We all have to support one another, so please don't do that. Again, let your budget and other resources decide what you can and cannot do.
I have had great results with the following resources but you can also do a Google search of "plays for kids":

- **The Broadway Jr collection.** These junior versions of Broadway plays are made so easy to direct and perform! They come with CD backing tracks (no band required), Director's and Production guides and as many scripts as you need. They are costly, however if you gear your program towards this type of production, you can add in the costs to the fees. For the U.S. these shows can be found at mtishows.com/broadway-junior and for NZ/AUS, they can be found at www.halleonard.com/broadwayjunior/60min/index.jsp
- **12 Fabulously Funny Fairy Tale Plays.** This is a far more cost effective option. No royalty or photocopy fees required, just the cost of the book. There are several books in this series and I've used plays from all of them. The scripts are basic and it comes with a teaching guide and learning activity. These can be found at Amazon.com.

3) **The Schedule.** Once you have decided on WHAT, WHERE and WHEN you will be performing, make a rehearsal and performance schedule (keep in mind that if you change dates, you may need to inform the company you are paying royalties to).

The follow sample rehearsal schedule is based on a 10-week term with a two-day-per-week class, each class being one hour long. I have also based this on a musical production of *Alice in Wonderland* which has a production time of 30 minutes and is divided into two acts, each containing five scenes and five songs.

Keep in mind that if you are going to put on a show like this, you will need to dedicate ALL class time to rehearsing as per the schedule and would have no time for games, lessons or exercises but I do ALWAYS suggest starting with a warm-up to get everyone focused.

I've included volunteer days where you will need help to build and paint the set, as well as a day for lighting and sound. You can also include a day for costumes or props or anything else you need but be careful not to burn parents and volunteers out. This goes back to your resources – a sheet asking parents what skills they are willing to contribute would be a great way to begin planning these days. Better yet, when the kids sign up, ask the parents to volunteer for a pre-determined volunteer day. Throw in some snacks and drinks and most will be more than happy to oblige.

NOTE: For anything longer than a 30-minute performance, you will need a minimum of two, two-hour-long rehearsals per week for at least 10 weeks in order to pull off a decent show.

Rehearsal Schedule for Alice in Wonderland

Week	SUN	MON	TUES	WED	THURS	FRI	SAT
1		First Read		Assign Parts Act 1: Learn 1st 2 songs.			
2		Go over 1st 2 songs. Learn nxt 3. Scenes 1-3		Go over songs. Scenes 1-4			
3		Choreograph songs 1-3		Scenes 5 Practice songs 1-3			
4		Choreograph songs 4 & 5 Scenes 4 & 5		Run through first act			
5		Costume Fittings6		Act 2: Learn songs 6,7,8 Act 2, Sn 1-3			
6		Go over songs 6-8. Act2, Sn 3-5		Learn songs 9& 10. go over Act 2, Sns 1-3			
7		Choreograph songs 6-8.		Scenes 1-3 Practice songs 6 &8			Volunteer set building day.
8		Choreograph songs 9 & 10 Scenes 4 & 5		Run through Act 2			
9		Run through Act 1		Run through Act 2			Volunteer lighting/ sound Day
10		Run through Act 1		Run through Act 2	Dress rehearsal 6-9 All Volunteers and Cast.	5:00 Call Performance 6:30 pm	

4) **Read and Write.** Okay so now you've got your resources, your venue, your performance dates, your play and your schedule – time to start making notes. First, make sure you thoroughly READ the play you are about to start directing. This might seem like a no-brainer, but I have dealt with more than a couple of directors who appeared to have only skimmed through the script we were working on (I must admit that I have also been guilty of this myself, but it's not something I would do again!) This makes things frustrating for the actors, even young actors, whose thoughts are on different aspects of the performance than the director – because usually the director is caught up with the performance as a whole, while the individual actors are more focused on their individual parts.

Make notes in your – The Director's – script on anything that comes to mind while reading it. I always tell my classes that at the end of a production, a script should look absolutely mutilated…unless you are renting scripts, in which case, it should be written only in pencil and then erased. This is NOT an option I would ever consider with children however! For my classes, I carried around a stapler for falling-off pages, and tape for torn ones.

5) **The Big Meeting.** Prior to starting rehearsals, I would highly recommend holding a parents and students meeting. In fact, I would make this mandatory as it sets the expectations and tone for what's about to unfold. This step may be dealt with via a newsletter if the Big Show isn't going to be so big, or if you are just holding an end-of-term recital. However, for the classes that are geared toward productions, a parent/student meeting is very important.

- This is where you'll set out your vision – so make it sound inviting and fun, while also reiterating that it is also a lot of hard work. Set out your expectations for behavior and commitment – going over the "Safety, Respect, Fun" rules would be excellent here.
- Ask for help! This is the perfect opportunity to begin amassing your resources.

- Hand out the schedule and ask for everyone to make sure they are available on Dress rehearsal and Performance dates and if there are any other significant times when their children might be away.
- Explain the process. For me, I always explained to parents and students that EVERY role, no matter how big or small, in a production is crucial to the success of the production. There is a saying in the "Biz": "There are no small roles, only small actors", meaning that even the smallest role, with the least lines, can steal the show if the actor is totally committed to that part. I usually have lots of funny examples to give, like the one where a boy playing a mouse in *Cinderella* was so committed to his twitching mouse face as he scuttled across the stage, that he actually got a standing ovation at the end of the play and no other actor did – not even the girl who played Cinderella.

6) The first day of rehearsals is always **The First Read-Through**. Sitting in a circle, everyone should have a copy of the script. I usually go around and assign people parts to read in order of appearance until everyone has had a turn to read something – it doesn't matter which parts they might want at this point; it's just about reading the script. I explain that the purpose of the read-through is to read the story, and to start to imagine what it might look like on stage.

Depending on how long the play is, this can become tiresome, so have a couple of movement-oriented warm-ups or exercises to break up the monotony of reading. With younger kids, this can get especially hard when they're having trouble reading. Don't be afraid to jump in and help to move things along.

7) **Assigning parts is the hardest part!** Oh my gosh, I wish there was an easier way to do this, but there just isn't. I always reiterate that every single part to a play is just as important as the next – the lighting person, the sound person, the wardrobe person, the person who organizes the props are all equally important to a production as the "lead" actor. In fact, I don't use that word except to discount it. It's

good to stress that everyone is responsible for a great production and no one is allowed to put down anyone for the role they are given. After saying that, I usually say – "So, do we all agree that whatever you get, is what you get and you won't throw a fit?" If they agree, I continue to dish out the parts. There WILL be disappointment, but that is not your issue. If the parents were at your meeting, then they will be able to explain to their child how best to deal with the disappointment.

8) **Stick to your schedule!** If your schedule is realistic – and the only way to know is to look at mine, which has been tested and to do a bit of research by looking at other schedules on the internet – then you should be alright. However, don't forget to be FLEXIBLE!
   If for any reason thing get behind, don't panic. I always made sure that I didn't neglect the second half of any production. This is a biggie. In the beginning I learned this the hard way and would get stuck on the first Act, trying to perfect it before moving on. It's better for the cast to semi-know the whole play than to know half of it perfectly and the ending (which is sometimes the most important part of the story) not at all.

9) **Focus on the story!** If you keep the cast focused on the story, rather than his or her individual parts, then, if someone forgets a line or a cue, they should be able to improvise if they know what's supposed to happen next. Tell the younger ones not to worry so much about the exact words they need to say and to pay more attention to what's going on in the scene. For older actors this is called "presence" or being present within a scene rather than being in "your head" worrying about what you're supposed to say or do next.
   Sometimes, as a warm-up, I would have the class do a silly summary of the play. In a circle, we would tell the story of the play we were performing as a game where each student tells a small bit, then passes it on to the next person by saying, "And then…". This helps them to establish the sequence of events so they can remember what is supposed to happen next if they need to improvise anything.

10) **Costume time!** Getting into costume can really help kids feel their character and can ramp up the momentum of any play. It can also

create a major distraction, expense and headache if you don't have help. As mentioned, I owned a costume hire business as well as the drama workshops and they complimented each other brilliantly. However, without this resource, I would have had to flag the elaborate costumes and settle for a bit of this and that. Here are some costume tips:

- Enlist parents to source their child's costume. Be sure to be specific about each child's requirements so that parents don't spend money unnecessarily. Also, try to make the requirements as 'free' or 'affordable' as possible. If a parent is having trouble sourcing an item, be sure to tell them it's not a problem but to let you know early so that you can source it yourself.
- Second-hand shops are GREAT sources for costumes. Always try these first before paying big bucks!
- Go minimalist! I have had great success with minimal effort in the past. Not only do busy parents appreciate it, but you'd be surprised how far a small bit of costuming can go. Sometimes just a bit of face paint is all you need to tell the audience someone is a villain or a monkey or one of the three pigs. One item of clothing or even just a hat can also communicate character to the audience.

11) **Give 'em Props!** 'Props' is the theatrical term for 'properties' or things an actor uses to tell the story. A table and chair are part of the 'Set' while a walking cane and a basket of goodies are 'props'. Actors need to get used to using whatever props they'll be using as soon as possible so I usually try to source these from the beginning.

Actors are responsible for keeping track of their own props and should have a special place for them when they are finished using them. I also tell the students to keep their hands off other people's props – I'd say, "Hands off O.P.P." and they'd say "Yeah you know me"...most of them, and maybe most of you are too young to know the reference to the 90s hip hop song, but I got a kick out of it.

12) **All the world's a stage.** To stage or not to stage, that is the question. As mentioned earlier, you do not need an elevated stage but if you do have one, be sure it is safe! That said, what you will be using as the backdrop or the **SET** to your story must also be safe and practical. It's all very well to have an actual balcony for Juliet to call to her Romeo from, but ensure that whomever is building it is qualified, and that it is not going to endanger your cast.

I am a minimalist and love for the audience to use their imaginations as well as the cast. For my after-school shows, we used cardboard sets which the students helped to paint. Just about anything can be made from cardboard and it's free!

For my high school productions, we usually had to build a thing or two. I once 'implied' an entire house by just hanging a window frame from the ceiling. It was very effective (until a gust of wind from an open door started it swinging).

Cheap paint and lots of cardboard were my sets of choice!

13) **Let there be light!** Once again, you do not have to go big budget on lighting. Of course all the beautiful colors, fog machines, spot lights

and strobes are neat, but they are really expensive! It's not just the lights that cost, but the expertise of the person running them. Unless you have a parent who is also a lighting expert, I'd suggest you stick to basic spot lights (spots) which you can hire from an event lighting company or stand up spots, which can usually be hired from any party rental.

If you do have a budget for an elaborate lighting plan, be sure to have a tech rehearsal with the person who will be operating the lights prior to the real thing! This will help to work out any bugs and will hopefully avoid awkward scene changes.

14) **The sound…of silence.** All the hard work of you, your actors and your volunteers can be for naught if your audience can't hear what's going on. Sometimes, no matter how much 'projection' a kid can muster is not enough to allow the folks in the back row to hear their little darling. Again, this comes down to budget. Lighting and sound can eat up the largest portion of production costs in my experience and should only be used if they have to be.

Usually a few microphones on the stage should be enough to pick up sound, but if your venue is very large you may need to think about mic packs for each individual actor.

In addition to hearing the actors on stage, sound is used for playing accompanying music, sound effects and voice-overs. If your production requires any of the above, you will need a PC system and a way to play your sounds like a laptop, iPod, or stereo.

As with the lighting, sound can also be tricky to operate. Getting a volunteer to specifically focus on sound cues, volume levels and making sure all the mic packs are on when they're supposed to be and OFF when they're supposed to be is crucial! (There's nothing worse than someone leaving a mic pack on, going back stage and accidentally telling the whole audience that they farted on stage!)

15) **Dress Rehearsal – The Test!** Technically there should be what is called a "Tech Rehearsal" before the Dress Rehearsal. Tech rehearsals are only for larger productions and involve a run-through of all the 'Tech' stuff. I'm making the assumption that most people who are reading this book are going to start off with something a bit more manageable,

but if you've gone for the Big Time, then hey, you are a brave brave soul!

I tell my students that they should treat Dress Rehearsal just like it was the real thing. No stopping, no laughing, no messing around backstage. If something does go wrong – and it most likely will – it's best to just make a note of what happened and help the kids to move on.

The reality is that sometimes everybody forgets a line, even professional actors – what makes them professional is that they carry on no matter what, and no matter how badly they may have messed up, they cover it up on stage so that the audience doesn't even know anything happened. Again, **Fake It Till You Make It!**

At the end of Dress Rehearsal – which is usually a very exhausting night (or day), I usually sit everyone down and tell each one individually what a fantastic job they did. I will have made notes on little things that each person did or said that was particularly wonderful and that contributed to making our story a success. This includes the volunteers who have helped in any way throughout the 'season' (a 'season' is the term for a production from beginning to end). If there are things that people need to work on, I will hand these out too – but gently. It's already a big thing to put yourself out there – to be up on stage in front of people is not something that everyone can do. In fact, speaking in front of people is deemed one of the most frightening things for a large portion of the population. It's best to remember that anyone who risks getting up in front of an audience is a very brave individual indeed and that person's brave soul should be kept intact at all times. Therefore, my other mantra: Always elevate and encourage, sometimes give pointers – be careful not to criticize – never EVER crush.

16) **Break a Leg - The Big Show!!** If you've ever wondered why actors say "Break a leg" instead of "Good luck", you might know by the end of your first show. Theater practitioners are very superstitious for good reason. Murphy's Law is rife in the world of theater. If anything can go wrong, it most likely will go wrong, which is why planning for contingency is so important! "Break a Leg" is said because if you are

told to break a leg in theater, you won't. However, if you are told to have "Good Luck", you won't have that either…as the theory goes. It is just silly superstition, but just you wait and see! Don't worry though, it will be fine…I mean…break a leg!

Now, just before The Big Show, you might notice the kids are starting to act a bit strange. Some may be oddly quiet, others may be emotional, and some may be bouncing off the walls more than usual. It's probably nerves. Everyone gets nervous. It's a normal and natural reaction to taking risk. Once I made the mistake of telling my students about PSPs (Pre-show Pees and Poos). You see, I was trying to make light of a scary situation in which at least two students were feeling so sick to their stomachs that they didn't think they could perform.

I said, "Oh, you're perfectly normal. You're just having the PSPs."

To which all the students replied, "What are PSPs?"

"Oh, all actors get PSPs" I said, "It's normal – but it's not very nice."

"Well? What are they?" They repeated.

At this point I was thinking, "Oh no, I've really backed myself into a corner – what if the parents don't appreciate me talking about pees and poos." But I had put myself in this place, so I committed.

"PSPs, stand for…" I lowered my voice and looked around very dramatically like I was about to tell them all a big secret, "Pre-show pees and poos."

They erupted with laughter.

I said, "It's true. Actors can get so nervous that their tummies bubble and bubble and it feels like there's a million butterflies in there. Then suddenly, you have to go to the bathroom. It happens to me a lot."

Still laughter. Then almost all the kids said that that's how they felt, and we had a big, fun conversation about nerves and tummies and of course, pees and poos. I stressed that it was important that they went to the bathroom before they went on stage so that they could concentrate on the story and not on having "to go".

Well, I say that this was a mistake because of course when the parents arrived to pick up the kids that's all they could talk about and I worried it would be taken out of context. So, before the Big Show I told the whole audience about PSPs and it was well received (by most)…in hindsight, I think I'd rather have just mentioned the part about the butterflies.

But I digress.

The Big Show should be about accomplishment and celebrating hard work. Everyone should know that they've all done their best and whatever happens on "The Night" will happen. Most likely the audience will love it and the kids will bask in the applause at the end, which usually seals the deal for most young actors – that is where they become hooked. Entertaining people is a gift, and once you realize you can give people that gift, it's such an incredible feeling that you just want to keep doing it!

BREAK A LEG!

Your First 10 Lessons

The following lessons are geared towards ages six to 13+, and are meant to build upon one another. It is not crucial that they be kept in order, however I would suggest that they are as much as possible. In addition, these lessons are one-hour long. If you are wishing to have an end-of-term show based on these lessons, I would suggest that you have a couple of games of Space Jump! and a few other demonstrations rather than anything scripted as I have not allowed for extra rehearsal time. Parents love to see what the kids have been doing in class and Space Jump! is always loads of fun. You can even get the parents to have a try if they're willing!

Remember to also have a couple of spare games at the ready in case something doesn't go as planned. Here is a list of things you'll need before starting:

- A bell or other gentle noisemaker to call everyone to the circle and to start and stop games
- A music playing device
- Balls of different shapes and sizes (not hard like baseballs though)
- A few soft toys
- Chairs

Lesson 1

1) **Meet and Greet:**
   Time: Approximately 5 minutes
   Sitting in a circle start by introducing yourself and give a brief synopsis of what you will be doing (i.e. getting to know each other, having an important business meeting, then playing some fun games, learning a little bit about acting, etc.) Be sure to emphasize that participation is voluntary and that anyone can say "pass" if they would rather wait until they're feeling more comfortable.
2) **The Name Game** – Under **Warm-Ups in The Stuff**
   Time: Approximately 10 minutes.

3) **The Business Meeting** – Refer to **Step 6: The Rules or The Business Meeting**
   Time: Approximately 10 – 15 minutes.
4) **Exercise: Hello**– Under **Exercises in The Stuff**
   Time: Approximately 10 minutes
5) **Lesson: What do we know about Drama?**
   Time: Approximately 5-7 minutes
   Sitting in a circle, ask the question, "What do we know about Drama?" I start by saying "I want to know what you already know about Drama or what you think it is. Don't worry, there is no right or wrong answer for this." This can be explored either by allowing students to raise their hands and give their answer (don't encourage shouting out answers or you will end up with chaos) or by saying "Drama is…" and go around the circle until everyone has had a chance.
   Take time to validate every answer. If someone says "I don't know", you can reply, "That's okay because we're about to find out!"
   I usually end by adding what I think Drama is and that is: STORYTELLING! Telling stories with our whole selves using our Voices, our Bodies, our Movements and our Space!
6) **Exercise: Many Ways to Open a Door!** – Under **Exercises in The Stuff**
   Time: Approximately 10 minutes.
7) **End of Lesson 1 Recap.**
   Time: 5 minutes.
   Be sure to leave time for this recap and gather everyone to the circle. Recap briefly what you did and what you will do next time.
   Homework: Ask the students to pay attention to how people use their Voices and Bodies when they tell stories – even when it's just a story about something that happened during the day. Ask them to make a mental note about what part of the story they found most interesting and why.

Lesson 2

1) **Meet and Greet:**
   Time: Approximately 3 minutes
   I usually start the second lesson with a quick hello, how is everybody and then straight into a warm-up game to re-familiarize us all with each other.
2) **Warm-up: Name Ball** – Under **Warm-ups in The Stuff**
   Time: Approximately 5 minutes
3) **Warm-up: What are you doing?** – Under **Warm-ups in The Stuff**
   Time: Approximately 10 minutes
4) **Lesson: What is the main goal for an actor?**
   Time: Approximately 10-15 minutes
   Sitting in a circle, recap that last week you explored the meaning of Drama and that this week we are going to look at one of the parts of Drama: The Actor. I ask, "What do you think the main goal for an actor is? Once again, don't worry, there is no right or wrong answer for this."
   Okay, so be aware that you might get some verryyyy interesting answers for this one. Some kids might say, "The main goal for an actor is to become famous", or "The main goal for an actor is to make all the other actors look bad" – these are real answers I have had, so it's best to go into this prepared and with a sense of humor. I usually always challenge an answer like these with questions and will never EVER say, WRONG or NO...you can't, as you've already told them there's no right or wrong.
   However, I will answer with, "If an actor's main goal is to become famous, and I'm sure that's a goal that MANY actors have, then how do you think that actor will become famous? In other words, what will he or she have to do on the stage that will make people take notice?"
   See what I did there? Take it back to teamwork and telling the story. If someone says that an actor's main goal is to "Make all the other actors look bad" you can do the same thing by asking "How would this help the actor to tell the story to the audience?" They'll soon figure it out, just be careful not to degrade an answer...unless someone gives you an

inappropriate answer like "An actor's main goal is to kill all the other actors" (again, a real example)...have a sense of humor but move these kinds of answers along swiftly by saying something like "Well, a one-person show might be quite boring to the audience".

I end with my answer, which may not be the best: "I think an actor's main goal is to help to tell the story to the audience in the best way possible so that the audience somewhat believes the actor is the character they are playing and that they can really understand and appreciate the meaning of the story."

5) Exercise: Help Desk – Under Exercises in The Stuff
   Time: Approximately 10-15 minutes
6) Game: Mr. Hit – Under Games in The Stuff
   Time: Approximately 10 minutes
7) End of Lesson 2 Recap.
   Time: 5 minutes.
   Be sure to leave time for this recap and gather everyone to the circle. Recap briefly what you did and what you will do next time.
   Homework: Ask students to pay attention to the way people walk. Have them follow a parent or brother or sister around for a little while until they "perfect" that person's walk. If a child is unable to walk, suggest that they mimic something else their chosen person does like brush their teeth, chew their food, or use hand gestures when speaking.

Lesson 3

1) **Meet and Greet:**
   Time: Approximately 3 minutes
   Everybody should be familiar with each other now. Greet the class and let them know what you'll be doing today.
2) **Warm-up: Pinocchio** – Under **Warm-ups** in **The Stuff**
   Time: Approximately 5 minutes
3) **Warm-up: What are you doing?** – Under **Warm-ups** in **The Stuff**
   Time: Approximately 10 minutes
   Even though you did this game last week, it's good to repeat it as during the week the kids would have thought about other things they could do to make it more fun and interesting.
4) **Lesson: What tools does the actor use to act out a story?**
   Time: Approximately 10-15 minutes
   Sitting in a circle, recap that last week you explored the main goal of the actor and that this week we are going to look at Actors' Tools. I ask "What tools do you think an actor might use to tell the story when he or she is on the stage? Once again, don't worry, there is no right or wrong answer for this."
   When kids hear 'tools' they might start thinking about actual tools like hammers and saws. This might lead them to say things like "swords" or "costumes" or "hammers" or "saws". All of these answers would be right, in the right context, so again, validate the answers and start to steer them into thinking about 'tools' that we have with us all the time. I start to refine the question by asking, "What tool, that an actor has all the time, could he or she use to TELL the story, and SHOW the story?"
   I end with my answer, which may not be the best: "I think that an actor can use many different types of tools to help him or her tell a story to the audience, but I'm an actor and I would say that my most valuable tools are my Voice and my Body. I can change how my voice sounds to show that I'm young or old, angry or sad, excited or worried – and the same with my body. The way I stand or move, shows the audience what kind of person I might be, and how that person is feeling."
5) **Exercise: Walking Like...** – Under **Exercises** in **The Stuff**

Time: Approximately 10-15 minutes

6) **Game: Directions** – Under Games in The Stuff
   Time: Approximately 10 minutes

7) **End of Lesson 3 Recap.**
   Time: 5 minutes.
   Be sure to leave time for this recap and gather everyone to the circle. Recap briefly what you did and what you will do next time.
   Homework: Ask students to think of four emotions and see if they can catch themselves experiencing these emotions in a mirror. For instance, if their little brother or sister makes them angry – then, instead of yelling at the brother or sister, run to a mirror and see what angry looks like on their face.

Lesson 4

1) **Meet and Greet:**
   Time: Approximately 3 minutes
   Greet the class and let them know what you'll be doing today.
1) **Warm-up: Group juggle** – Under **Warm-ups in The Stuff**
   Time: Approximately 5 minutes
2) **Game: Space Jump!** – Under **Games in The Stuff**
   Time: Approximately 15-20 minutes
   This game takes a little time to explain and understand, but once they get it, it will become a favorite. I found this to be the most requested Drama game of all time!
3) **Lesson: Move it! Move it!**
   Time: Approximately 10-15 minutes
   Sitting in a circle, recap that last week you explored the main goal of the actor and that this week we are going to look at Actors' Tools. I ask "What are some different ways an actor can move on stage?"
   This can be a really fun lesson, but be careful not to let it go too long exploring all the different ways. Ideally, you want the students to "show" you their answers rather than "tell" you. So, you can line them up on the side of the stage or the area you will be using as the stage. They should each think of a different way to move across the stage.
   At this point, you do not need to get them to think of any motivation or emotion behind the movement, just get them to move. You'll see tip-toes, leaps, running, jumping, skipping, dancing...try to encourage them to use levels, as in crouching, slithering or pretending to have a broken leg.
   Keep in mind the "safety" aspect of Drama – you don't want kids spinning across the stage and onto the floor.

   At the end of the lesson, you can do a summary of all the ways people moved across the stage. Be sure to point out the different LEVELS they were at when they did their movement. If some were crawling, then they were at a lower LEVEL than ones who were walking, but some might have been jumping and going in between a high level and a medium level.

Also point out the pace in which people were moving – some were fast, some were slow, some might have even been in slow motion.

4) **Exercise: Flocking** – Under Exercises in The Stuff
   Time: Approximately 10-15 minutes
5) **Game: Directions** – Under Games in The Stuff
   Time: Approximately 10 minutes
   You may have played this last week, but this week feel free to add at least two new Directions.
6) **End of Lesson 4 Recap.**
   Time: 5 minutes.
   Be sure to leave time for this recap and gather everyone to the circle. Recap briefly what you did and what you will do next time.
   Homework: Ask students take a normal thing that they do every day, like brush their teeth, or make their lunch, and to slooowwwww it down into super slow motion. Tell them to pay attention to every little movement.

Lesson 5

1) **Meet and Greet:**
   Time: Approximately 3 minutes
   Greet the class and let them know what you'll be doing today.
2) **Warm-up: Bippity Bippity Bop** – Under Warm-ups in The Stuff
   Time: Approximately 5 minutes
3) **Game: Space Jump!** – Under Games in The Stuff
   Time: Approximately 15-20 minutes
   You played this last week, but it's a good idea to play it again so the kids can get a better handle on it. Plus, it gives them the much loved stage time.
4) **Lesson: Space! The Final Frontier!**
   Time: Approximately 10-15 minutes
   Sitting in a circle, recap that last week you explored the many ways actors move on stage. This week you will be focusing on SPACE – not outer space, but the space you are playing in, the space between characters and space between the actors and the audience. Ask the students, "How do actors use space?" This is a broad question, be sure to tell them you don't mean outer space, but space on stage, space between their character and other characters, between them and the audience and so on.
   After they've thought about it and have given some answers, you can show them some ways to use space with the following exercise.
5) **Exercise: Elevator** – Under Exercises in The Stuff
   Time: Approximately 10 minutes
6) **Game: Slow Motion Races/Olympics** – Under Games in The Stuff
   Time: Approximately 10 minutes
7) **End of Lesson 5 Recap.**
   Time: 5 minutes.
   Be sure to leave time for this recap and gather everyone to the circle. Recap briefly what you did and what you will do next time.
   Homework: Ask students to think about a time when they felt like they couldn't do something and they were getting frustrated – like trying to ride a bike, or catch a piece of popcorn with their mouth. How did

they accomplish their goal? If they didn't, what do they think they need to do in order to accomplish it?

Lesson 6

1) **Meet and Greet:**
   Time: Approximately 3 minutes
   Greet the class and let them know what you'll be doing today.
2) **Warm-up: HA!** – Under Warm-ups in The Stuff
   Time: Approximately 5 minutes
3) **Game: Slow Motion Races/Olympics** – Under Games in The Stuff
   Time: Approximately 10 minutes
4) **Lesson: Mime**
   Time: Approximately 10-15 minutes
   Sitting in a circle, recap that last week you explored how we use Space in Drama and that this week we are going to explore Mime! Ask the students, "What do you think of when you hear the word 'mime'?" You can ask for verbal answers first – again, always remember to validate all answers. After they kids have 'said' everything about 'mime' get them to 'show' you some things. One of the most common things that kids will show about mime is the 'box'.
   Remind them that they have done mime in class already when they played "What are you doing?" and maybe other games as well.
   Ask them, "What makes a mime act more effective or enjoyable for the audience?"
   While I'm not sure what type of answers you'll get here, you can guide them toward "using their whole body" to act a scene. For instance, if they are trying to mime walking a large dog, they will need to use 'tension', gestures...like wiping sweat off their brow and finger pointing at the naughty dog, levels – where the dog might be getting the better of them and so on. You can ask them, "How will the audience know your dog is bigger than you?"
5) **Exercise: Many Ways to Open a Door** – Under Exercises in The Stuff
   Time: Approximately 10 minutes
6) **Game: Charades** – Under Games in The Stuff
   Time: Approximately 10 minutes
7) **End of Lesson 6 Recap.**
   Time: 5 minutes.

Be sure to leave time for this recap and gather everyone to the circle. Recap briefly what you did and what you will do next time.

Homework: Ask students to eat a piece of lemon or something sour, if they get a chance – and to pay attention to the taste, the smell, the texture and the sound they make when they eat it.

Lesson 7

1) **Meet and Greet:**
   Time: Approximately 3 minutes
   Greet the class and let them know what you'll be doing today.
2) **Warm-up: Circle Dance** – Under **Warm-ups in The Stuff**
   Time: Approximately 5 minutes
3) **Warm-up: Yes, Let's!** – Under **Warm-ups in The Stuff**
   Time: Approximately 10 minutes
4) **Lesson: The Senses**
   Time: Approximately 15-20 minutes
   Sitting in a circle, recap that last week you explored Mime by using our bodies to tell stories. This week we are going to explore the senses! Ask, "Does anyone know what the senses are? Give me just one please." Go around until all five (or six) senses are mentioned. Then discuss how an actor might show a certain reaction to a certain sense when it's not really there. For instance, if an actor pretends to touch something very hot, how can she or he show how hot it is and how much it hurt when there isn't actually anything hot to touch?
   After students have given their answers, hand out one napkin to each student. Then hand out one slice of lemon to each students, asking them only to look at the slices and smell them for now. They will start to get excited so tell them to pay attention to what is happening in their mouths. Are they watering? Are they feeling nervous about eating a lemon because they already know it's going to be sour? What does nervousness feel like?
   Then, ask them to smell the lemon. What does it smell like?
   Next ask them to taste it. This is the fun part. Be sure to have them look around at each other's faces when they do this.
   When everyone has tasted the lemon, pass out a small marsh mellow each (Note: be sure to get parents' permission before giving children ANY food in case of allergies or intolerances, make substitutions as needed).
   Do the same with the marsh mellow, first have them smell it and ask them if their mouths are watering. Finally, have them taste it – again,

looking around. What do other kids' faces look like when they're eating the marsh mellow and how is it different to when they ate the lemon?

Give them one more small marsh mellow each for doing such a great job!

5) **Exercise: Walking like… – Under Exercises in The Stuff**
   Time: Approximately 10 minutes
   You've done this one before but it should have new depth now that they've explored the Senses.

6) **Game: Space Jump! – Under Games in The Stuff**
   Time: Approximately 10 minutes

7) **End of Lesson 7 Recap.**
   Time: 5 minutes.
   Be sure to leave time for this recap and gather everyone to the circle. Recap briefly what you did and what you will do next time.
   Homework: Ask students to pay attention to how people use their hands when they talk.

Lesson 8

1) **Meet and Greet:**
   Time: Approximately 3 minutes
   Greet the class and let them know what you'll be doing today.
2) **Warm-up: Bippity Bippity Bop** – Under **Warm-ups** in The Stuff
   Time: Approximately 5 minutes
3) **Game: Mister Hit (Pirate Style)** – Under Games in The Stuff
   Pirate style means having everyone do a Pirate accent and take on a Pirate name!
   Time: Approximately 7 minutes
4) **Lesson: Gestures**
   Time: Approximately 15-20 minutes
   Sitting in a circle, recap that last week you explored The Senses and how actors are able to pretend to feel, see, hear, taste or smell something that isn't really there. This week we are going to explore Gestures! Ask, "Does anyone know what a gesture is?" Go around and have students give examples of gestures, which can be anything that says something without words using a part of your body. For example, thumbs up means "okay" or "All good" and thumbs down means the opposite. Raised eyebrows can mean concern or surprise while lowered eyebrows can mean that someone is not happy. Pointing a finger can be showing someone the direction to go in, while wagging a finger can mean "No, no, no!"
   Ask student to show gestures for the following words and sentences:
   - I don't know.
   - What's going on here?
   - It's over there.
   - Oh, yes please!
   - No, thank you.
   - Come on.
   - Hurry up!
   - Go away!
   - Stop!
   - I love this pie!

- Yuck, no more of that please!
- I'm okay, thanks.
- Shhhh! We're in a library.

5) **Game: Machines** – Under Exercises in The Stuff
   Time: Approximately 10 minutes
6) **Game: Where are we?** – Under Games in The Stuff
   Time: Approximately 10 minutes
7) **End of Lesson 8 Recap.**
   Time: 5 minutes.
   Be sure to leave time for this recap and gather everyone to the circle. Recap briefly what you did and what you will do next time.
   Homework: Ask students to pay attentions to all the sights and sounds of a particular place, like the beach, or a barber shop. Can they name ten different sounds?

Lesson 9

1) **Meet and Greet:**
   Time: Approximately 3 minutes
   Greet the class and let them know what you'll be doing today. Also, this might be the second to last class so be sure to remind the class if there will be a performance and if so, what you'll be doing and when it will be. A notice home at week 8, 9 and 10 are advised.

2) **Warm-up: What are you doing?** – Under **Warm-ups** in The Stuff
   Time: Approximately 5 minutes

3) **Game: Help Desk** – Under Games in The Stuff
   Time: Approximately 10 minutes

4) **Lesson: The Voice!**
   Time: Approximately 15-20 minutes
   Sitting in a circle, recap that last week you explored Gestures and how actors are able to use certain parts of their body to say a lot without using words. This week we are going to explore The Voice! Ask, "Why do you think we waited to explore this actor's tool, The Voice, last?" Again, you might get a range of answers and this time there is a bit of a right answer, which is the fact that most new or young actors tend to rely on The Voice to TELL the story, but in Drama, we try to SHOW the story as much as possible first.

   The Voice is important, but as the saying goes, "Acting without using THE WHOLE BODY, is like playing the piano with one finger".

   Ask, "Does anyone know what the word 'projection' means?" Have them think about a projector and what it does – it throws light and a picture onto a screen. If we 'project' our voices, we are basically throwing them onto something else. In the case of Drama, we are projecting our voices to the very back of the room so that everyone in the audience can hear us.

   Ask, "What else can we do with our voice to make the audience more interested in our story?"

   You might get answers like changing your character's voice, making it louder or softer, silly voices, accents and so on.

At the end I always say, "It's all very well to change your voice to fit a character, but if the audience can't understand what you're saying, you're not telling them the story and they will be confused about what's happening."

5) **Exercise: Soundscape** – Under Exercises in The Stuff
   Time: Approximately 10 minutes
6) **Game: The Party Game** – Under Games in The Stuff
   Time: Approximately 10 - 15 minutes
7) **End of Lesson 9 Recap.**
   Time: 5 minutes.
   Be sure to leave time for this recap and gather everyone to the circle. Recap briefly what you did and what you will do next time.
   Homework: Ask students to be sure to give their notices to their parents.

Lesson 10

1) **Meet and Greet:**
   Time: Approximately 3 minutes
   Greet the class and let them know what you'll be doing today. Also, if this is the final class you might want to thank everyone for a great term and to advise of what might happen next term. Also, if you are having an end-of-term performance be sure to remind students and parents of date and time. For the final lesson, I usually choose the favorite games from the term and focus on that most of the time.
2) **Warm-up: Popcorn** – Under Warm-ups in The Stuff
   Time: Approximately 5 minutes
3) **Game: Space Jump!** – Under Games in The Stuff
   Time: Approximately 15 minutes
4) **Lesson: The Actor's Tools: Voice, Body, Movement and Space – putting them all together!**
   Time: Approximately 15-20 minutes
   Sitting in a circle, recap all lessons you have learned so far this term. Tell the students that great acting is about putting all those tools together and building a character – then letting the characters show and tell the story.
   Discuss examples from the term when they think people used lots of tools at once to tell a story.
5) **Game: The Party Game** – Under Games in The Stuff
   Time: Approximately 10 minutes
   Kids love this game, so playing it two classes in a row will be a treat! You can even use this game in the end-of-term performance if you like.
6) **End of Lesson 10 Recap.**
   Time: 5 minutes.
   Be sure to leave time for this recap and gather everyone to the circle. Recap briefly what you did and what you will do next term.

The Stuff

The following Drama Warm-ups, Games and Exercises are not all my creations and most are known by many different names and have lots of variations. Drama is an art form that is always evolving and creating anew so, as you go along, you too will compile, create and collect the Warm-Ups, Games and Exercises that work best for you and your classes – adding your own variations to them here and there.

If you ever need more material, there is a treasure trove of ideas on the internet. Google Drama Games, Improv, Warm Ups or Ice breakers and you should have enough material to keep you going for years!

Enjoy!

Warm ups

1. 1 to 20

What: Counting to 20 one person at a time, but in no particular order. SYNCHRONIZATION, FOCUS, ENERGY

Techniques: VOICE, SPACE

How: In a circle, everyone should have their heads down and focusing on one spot on the ground. One person starts by saying "One", anyone in the circle can then say "two", then "three" and so on, but if more than one person says a number at the same time, the group must starts again at "One". The goal is to get to "twenty" without having to start again.

The secret to this game is becoming in tune with each other and not rushing it. I tell students to be okay with silence and to just enjoy the pauses.

I usually try three or four times, then move on to something else.

This is a great game to play when things have become chaotic or you're just about to go on stage.

2. Alien, Tiger, Cow

What: Think of Rock, Paper, Scissors using the whole body. ICE BREAKER. SYNCHRONIZATION.

Techniques: VOICE, BODY, MOVEMENT, SPACE

How: Everyone in a circle. There are three things that the players can be: Alien, Tiger or Cow. Aliens make antennae with their fingers and lean into the circle making the noise "zerp zeep zoop". Tigers lean into the circle making ferocious claws and roaring. The cows show off their udders by putting their hands on their bellies and mooing. The teacher or circle leader counts to three. On three everyone has to commit to one of the three characters: alien, tiger, or cow. Keep repeating the cycle of 1-2-3 until everyone does the same creature. This may never happen, but it's fun to try.

Change-ups: You can change the characters for anything as long as you all agree on the character gestures and noises. You can also play it as an elimination game by taking odd or even numbers out.

3. Bippity Bippity Bop

What: A person-in-the-middle circle game. Ice Breaker. Focus.

Techniques: VOICE, BODY, MOVEMENT, SPACE

How: Everyone into a circle with one person in the centre. The person in the middle of the circle starts to count to ten while spinning around. When they get to ten, they point to someone and say one of three things (there are other things you can add listed below):

   a) If the person-in-the-middle says "Bippity Bippity Bop", then the person pointed to has to say "Bop" before the person-in-the-middle does or he/she is "out" and has to change places with the person-in-the-middle.
   b) If the person-in-the-middle says "Elephant, Elephant one, two, three", then the person pointed at sticks their arm in front of their face and dangles it like an elephant trunk while making elephant noises. The people on either side of the "trunk person" must make the ears of the elephant. So the person on the left side uses their left arm to touch their head, and the person on the right uses their right arm to form the right ear. The elephant must be formed before the person-in-the-middle gets to "three". If the whole elephant doesn't come together by the time the person-in-the-middle gets to "three", then the person responsible for the non-elephant now becomes the person-in-the-middle
   c) If the person-in-the-middle says "Chicken, Chicken, one, two, three, four, five, six, seven, eight" then the person

pointed at has to do the "Chicken Dance" before the person-in-the-middle gets to "eight" – meanwhile, the rest of the group have to sing and clap the **"Chicken Dance Song"** (search this in YouTube if unfamiliar). If the person doing the chicken dance does any of the moves in the wrong order, then they have to trade places with the person-in-the-middle.

Change-ups: Feel free to make up your own challenges. Here in New Zealand we did one for the national rugby team the All Blacks where the person-in-the-middle called out "All Blacks, one, two, three". The person pointed at and their neighbours on either side had to form a "scrum" and say "hee" by the time the person-in-the-middle got to "three".

4. Circle Dance

What: Follow-the-leader meets Crazy dance moves in a circle! FUN, IMPROVISATION, MIRRORING

Techniques: BODY, MOVEMENT, SPACE

How: Everyone in a circle. Dance music is needed for this one. One person jumps into the middle of the circle and does a funny dance move, then everyone else does it too. Once everyone has had a turn in the middle – try to put all the moves together as a whole dance. This will devolve into complete craziness but it's about having fun and being silly.

5. Dude!

What: This is another synchronization warm up. LISTENING, SYNCHRONIZATION, FOCUS

Techniques: VOICE, BODY, SPACE

How: Get everyone into a tight circle and looking down at the ground. The teacher or the leader says, "One, two, three, Look!" Each player has to commit to whomever they're going to look at on "Look!" If players make eye contact, both yell "Dude!" and switch places. This is continued until a few people have been able to change places.

Change ups: You can play this with "outs" where the players who make eye contact move out of the circle and the game is continued until no players are left.

6. Everyone Who

What: A matching ice-breaking game. Designed to get people moving and interacting. ICE BREAKER

Techniques: VOICE, BODY, MOVEMENT, SPACE

How: Standing or sitting in a circle, one person in the middle is the Caller. There should be only enough spaces or chairs for the people on the outside of the circle as the Caller is "out". The Caller calls out a similarity, as in "Everyone who is wearing socks!", and everyone who happens to be wearing socks, including the Caller, all try to find a space. One person will be left over and is now the Caller (unless the previous Caller wasn't wearing socks and therefore didn't try to get a space, or wasn't fast enough).

The calling continues: Everyone who has been to Spain. If you are left handed, and so on until the game gets tiring.

7. Free Association

What: Saying whatever word pops into your mind. IMPROVISATION, QUICK THINKING, BEING SILLY

Techniques: VOICE

How: This is a great warm-up for improvisation and being silly. In a circle, one person starts off by saying any word. The person to her left (or right, doesn't matter which way you go) just says the first thing that comes to mind. People shouldn't try to say "something funny" or to think about the word that was said before. This is about being as random as possible and just letting thoughts fly free. If someone draws a blank, they should just say "blabadeblah" or some other nonsense word.

8. Group juggle

What: Juggling alone is hard enough, try doing it in a group! This is fun! Focus, Teamwork, Thinking

Techniques: VOICE, BODY, MOVEMENT, SPACE

How: Everyone in a circle. You will need about four or five things to juggle that are soft and safe. I suggest tennis balls, bouncy balls, and stuffed toys. It's more fun if the items are different sizes and textures. Start with tossing just one of the items around the circle. Before tossing an item to someone else, be sure to make eye contact with that person and call their name loudly. Slowly start to introduce the other items. This is where the need to have SOFT and SAFE juggling items becomes really important. When all four or five items are in play, it becomes necessary to make eye contact and call a person's name BEFORE tossing an item to them, otherwise, one poor person may end up getting pummeled by all items at once!

9. HA!

What: Pass the clap. This warm up is to get people listening, responding fast and reacting without thinking. Focus, Energy.

Techniques: VOICE, BODY, MOVEMENT, SPACE.

How: Everyone gets into a circle. One person in the circle turns to a person on their right or left, claps at them and loudly says "HA!" That person then passes the clap and "HA!" to the person next to them OR they may choose to clap and "HA!" back at the first person. The first person may not "ping-pong", that is clap back at the original person they clapped at or they are out. The Clap-"HA!" should go around the circle but can change direction at any time as long as players don't "ping-pong". This should be played fast and furiously, although with beginners it will be slow and clunky at first until they get the hang of it. People who stall, clap one way and "HA!" the other or ping-pong are out.

Change-ups: When a group really has the hang of the game, they can Clap-"HA!" across the circle but they MUST make eye-contact with the person they are passing to.

10. Hands

What: Moving energy around a circle by squeezing hands. FOCUS, TEAMWORK

Techniques: BODY, SPACE

How: This warm-up is to get everyone working together and focused. Everyone gets into a circle and joins hands. One person (usually the teacher to start) squeezes that hand that they are holding. The person that received the squeeze squeezes the hand of the person on the other side. This should start a hand squeeze that races around the circle. Someone else can start a squeeze going in the opposite direction, no one should know who or when the squeezes will occur until they get to their hand. This can erupt into hand-squeezing chaos if everyone tries to start a squeeze – so it is at the leader's discretion how many squeezers there can be at once.

Change ups: Add-ons to this warm up are fun! Add a sound pass, so one person passes a sound like "Beep" and the "Beep" goes around while the hand squeezes continue.

11. Jam Session

What: Using only mouths and bodies as instruments, a fun band is formed! IMPROVISATION, FUN, TIMING

Techniques: VOICE, BODY, MOVEMENT, SPACE

How: In a circle, one person makes a noise with their body or their mouth and repeats it. For example a simple four beat clap. The next person jumps in with another made-up sound while the first person continues to make their sound in time. The first two continue with their sounds, keeping the same rhythm while the next person joins in and so on. By the time you've gotten around the circle, the first couple of "jammers" might be pretty tired from keeping up their sounds the whole time, but the "band" will sound pretty great! If you want to keep it going by adding in solo parts, duets, trios and more, feel free! It's all about fun!

12. Name Ball

What: A beginning ice breaking and name-learning game. ICE BREAKER NAME LEARNING, TEAM BUILDING.

Techniques: VOICE, BODY, MOVEMENT, SPACE

How: Everyone is sitting or standing in a circle. You will need a soft ball. First, everyone should say their names, one at a time, clearly and loud enough to be heard. Then, one person calls another person by name, "Hi Jack!" then throws him the ball. That person says, "Thank you Jill", then calls to another person by name and so on. You can make this more fun and silly by adding accents or moods. For example, the teacher can call out "Sad" and the person holding the ball will have to change their voice and posture before throwing: "Excuse me Bob, but…" through sobs and sniffs, "would you please catch this ball?" Bob answers with tears in his eyes, "Why yes Gail, I would love to…waaaaaa".

13. Name Game

What: An ice breaker, name-learning, memory game that helps newcomers get to know each other better. ICE BREAKER, MEMORY, NAME-LEARNING, TEAM BUILDING

Techniques: VOICE, SPACE

How: Everyone sitting in a circle. The teacher or leader starts by saying their name plus one thing they like and one thing they dislike: "Hi! My name is Shauna. I like cats and I dislike pickles." The next person has to introduce the person before her/him say what that person likes and dislikes and then introduces her/himself and adds her/his like and dislike. Person number three has to recall the first two plus her/his own and so on. As it isn't really fair to make the tenth person remember EVERY person who came before, I usually start again at person number five.

14. Pass Catch

What: Passing silliness around a circle! IMPROVISATION

Techniques: VOICE, BODY, MOVEMENT, SPACE

How: Everyone gets into a circle with an arms-length distance between each other. The starter makes a bizarre gesture and sound and then "passes" these to the person on their right. That player immediately repeats back the gesture and noise, imitating the other player as best they can. They then create a new gesture and sound and it continues to be "passed" and "caught" around the circle. It is important that the players not stop to think in between passing or catching. Advanced players should receive, reflect, turn and create a new gesture and sound without pausing.

15. Ping Pong Poo

What: A quick-thinking word exercise. THINKING, FOCUS

Techniques: VOICE

How: Everyone sitting or standing in a circle. One person starts by saying "Ping", the next player says "Pong" and the next says "Poo". It continues around the circle very quickly and anyone who hesitates or says the wrong thing, or laughs at the word "poo" is out. This continues faster and faster until there is one person left.

16. Pinocchio

What: A story telling warm-up to get actors exploring how their bodies move...or don't move. TENSION, FOCUS, SENSATION

Techniques: VOICE, BODY, MOVEMENT, SPACE

How: Everyone standing (or sitting as needed) in a circle. The teacher guides the story of how Pinocchio slowly comes to life.

All the students start out pretending to be solid blocks of wood – so no movement and very tense.

The story: Today you are a piece of solid wood. A nice puppet maker named Gepetto found you in the woods and thought you would make a wonderful companion. Just as he started to think of all the wonderful ways he could make you come to life as a puppet, you had a thought! Your first thought, and since you were just a block of wood, thinking was all you could do (never mind that you didn't actually have a brain).

You thought, "This man is so nice, I wish I were really real like him, so we could be friends!"

Suddenly a blue light came down from the ceiling, you couldn't see it, but you could feel it. It felt happy. It was the beautiful Blue Fairy who granted you the wish of being real!

As Gepetto began to carve, you began to get very excited to see what would happen next. First, he carved your eyes…and POP! Your eyes opened WIDE! They looked around as much as they could.

Then he carved your ears. You could hear! But still you could only move your eyes, and your ears (for those who can wiggle their ears this is fun).

Next he carved your nose! You could smell for the first time and the whole house smelled like beautiful pine! You take a DEEP Breath, then wriggle your nose!

Now, Gepetto carves your mouth and WOW! You can speak! You say, "HI!", and "WOW!" You poke out your tongue and show your teeth.

Gepetto carves your head and neck next and you are amazed to be able to look to your right, and your left. You look up, and down. You look ALL AROUND!

Your right arm is next. Pop it goes, up and away from your body. Then your fingers on your right hand – they wiggle and point. You still don't have an elbow or wrist but those are next and WOW! What fun it is to have an arm.

The same thing happens with your left arm. Fingers next, then elbow, then wrist. Now both arms are going and it's fun to scratch your head and wave Hello!

Now Gepetto has carved your waist! You can twist and bend but you still don't have legs or feet!

The next thing to be carved are your toes. You wiggle and wiggle them, oh what fun!

Then you have feet and ankles, one, then the other...no legs yet and you're getting impatient, you feel like running!!!!

Finally, Gepetto carves your legs! First the right, then the left! BUT OH NO!

Gepetto is so tired, he has fallen asleep and you want to run...you try, but something feels funny.

What has Gepetto forgotten to carve? That's right! Your knees!!

Now it's time to have a no knees race!

**At this point I line all the students up, reminding them that they are wooden puppets with no knees, and they have a stiff-legged race. At the end of the race, Gepetto wakes up and carves their knees and they dance around the room, happy to be free and alive!

17. Popcorn

What: A fun warm-up to get the blood pumping! Focus, Energy

Technique: BODY, MOVEMENT, SPACE

How: Everyone gets into a circle. The goal of the game is to jump in the air and clap like popcorn. When enough people are jumping and clapping it sounds like popcorn popping! You can turn it into a game by eliminating players who jump and clap at the same time. If a player jumps at the same time as another player, but does not clap, then they're not out.

If players are stalling, tell them they'll burn...and if they stall for more than 5 seconds they're out.

18. Song Circle

What: Random singing about silly things. Improvisation

Techniques: VOICE

How: Everyone is in a circle. The person on the right of the starter chooses a general theme (love, travel, grocery items, household chores). Once the theme is chosen the starter starts to sing a random song about the theme chosen. Once the player gets stuck on the song, another player must show support and start to sing about the theme with a new song or a continuation of the starter's song. This continues until the song completely falls apart. New themes can be the start of new songs and it can continue until everyone has either had a turn or is totally sick of singing!

19. Stretching

What: Basic body stretches for physical Drama work. Physical, Body Focus

Technique: BODY, MOVEMENT, SPACE

How: Easy stretches to help everyone warm up their bodies and stay limber can also be fun when you're stretching things that don't normally get stretched like your nose, or your earlobes.

Ask each person to submit a "stretch" that everyone else then copies. Be sure to keep it safe and tell whomever is leading to please not do back bends or other difficult stretches (even if they consider it to be easy). The idea is to be silly, while also getting a good stretch.

20. Voice Warm-Up 1

What: A breath exercise to release tension in the voice.

Techniques: VOICE, BODY

How: Everyone in a circle standing or sitting straight. Ask them to take a normal breath in and then exhale. Make sure everyone's shoulders and chest are low and relaxed. Repeat many times making sure that your breaths are focused low in the abdomen by having everyone put on hand flat on the belly to feel it rise and fall. Be sure to go around the circle and help everyone to relax their shoulders and chest by tapping them on the shoulder if they're looking tense. Have students make an "s" sound like in hiss when they exhale.

21. Voice Warm-Up 2

What: A voice warm-up to release tension in the jaw during speaking and singing.

Techniques: VOICE, BODY

How: Place the heels of each hand directly below the cheek bone. Pushing in and down from the cheeks to the jaw, massage the facial muscles. Allow your jaw to passively open as you move the hands down the face. Repeat several times.

22. Voice Warm-Up 3

What: A voice warm-up to release lip tension and connects breathing and speaking.

Techniques: VOICE, BODY

How: Place your lips loosely together release the air in a steady stream to create a trill or raspberry sound. First try it on an "h" sounds. Then repeat on a "b" sound. Hold the sound steady and keep the air moving past the lips. Next try to repeat the b-trill gliding gently up and down the scales. Don't push beyond what it comfortable at the top or bottom of the scale.

23. Voice Warm-Up 4 – Tongue Trills

What: A voice warm-up to relax the tongue and help engage breathing and voice.

Techniques: VOICE, BODY

How: Exhale and trill your tongue with an "r" sound. Hold the sound steady and keep the breath connected. Now try to vary the pitch up and down the scale while trilling. Again, don't push beyond what is comfortable at the top or bottom of your scale.

24. Voice Warm-Up 5 – Two Octave Scales

What: A scale warm-up for the vocal folds.

Techniques: VOICE

How: Start in a low pitch and gently glide up the scale on a "me" sound. Don't push the top or bottom of your range but do try to increase the range gently each time you do the scales. Now reverse and glide down the scale from the top to the bottom on an "e" sound. You can try this on the "oo" sound also.

25. Voice Warm-Up 6 – Sirens

What: Improves the resonant focus of the sound and continues to stretch on the vocal folds.

Techniques: VOICE

How: Have the students pretend like they are sucking in spaghetti noodles. On exhalation, have them make a "woo" sound. It will be a buzz-like sound. Hold the sound steady for 2-3 attempts. Now use the woo sound to go up and down the scales.

26. Voice Warm-Up 7 - Humming

What: Relaxes your lips and highlights vibrations in your lips, teeth and facial bones.

Techniques: VOICE

How: Begin with lips gently closed with jaw released. Take an easy breath in and exhale while saying "hum". Begin with the nasal sound "mmm" and gently glide from a high to a low pitch as if you were sighing. Don't forget your vocal cool down after extensive vocal use. Gently humming feeling the focus of the sound on the lips is an excellent way to cool down the voice. You should hum gentle glides on the sound "m" feeling a tickling vibration in the lip/nose area.

27. Vocal Warm-Up 8 – Cool Down

What: After extensive vocal use, it's always advisable to cool down.

Techniques: VOICE

How: Gently humming feeling the focus of the sound on the lips is an excellent way to cool down the voice. You should hum gentle glides on the sound "m" feeling a tickling vibration in the lip/nose are.

28. What Are You Doing?

What: A fun miming warm-up or game to get the imagination going.
IMPROVISATION, FOCUS, LISTENING, ENERGY.

Techniques: VOICE, BODY, MOVEMENT, SPACE

How: Everyone gets into a circle. One player goes into the circle and starts to mime a simple activity. Once the activity has been established, one of the players from the circle jumps in and asks "what are you doing?" The player doing the mime has to tell a fib (lie) and respond with an activity that they are NOT doing. For example, if they are miming brushing their teeth, they might respond by saying "plucking a chicken". The player that asked "What are you doing?" has to being miming what the previous person has said (plucking a chicken). This continues until everyone has had a turn.

29. Yes, Let's!

What: A great improvisation warm-up to help actors to accept offers.
ACCEPTING, IMPROVISATION, ENERGY

Techniques: VOICE, BODY, MOVEMENT, SPACE

How: Everyone in a circle. Someone will loudly and very excitedly (I call it O.T.T. or Over the Top) suggest an activity for the group to mime ("Let's all do the hula!") Everyone simultaneously yells "Yes let's!", and starts the do the activity. Once the activity has been mimed the person on the right yells out something to mime, the group responds with an O.T.T. "Yes let's!" and starts the activity. For example, if someone calls out "Let's all ride horses!" The group responds with "Yes! Let's all ride horses!", and every manner of horse riding mime will begin (complete with sound effects). Then someone will suggest a new activity and the cycle continues.

Games

1. Alphabet Game

What: A scene game that relies on the actors' abilities to know their ABCs. IMPROVISATION, MEMORY, TEAMWORK

Techniques: VOICE, BODY, MOVEMENT, SPACE

How: This starts with three to four players in a scene. Someone from the audience chooses a topic for the scene. The players have to start each sentence within the scene with a consecutive letter of the alphabet...the first sentence starts with a word beginning with the letter A, the next sentence starts with a "B" word and so on. It is important to keep the scene active rather than just have a few actors standing still on a stage saying sentences. For example, a person in the audience chooses "The Zoo" as a topic. The players on the stage make quick choices about who they will be within the scene and the topic. Player 1 might say, "Alligators are my favorite animals at the zoo!" to which Player 2 might reply, "But we've already seen the alligators a million times. Can't we go see the gorillas?" Player 3 might decide that they are the parent in the situation and say, "Don't you two start fighting or we will go home. Every time we come to the zoo, you start in. First, we're going to see the bears!" At this point there should be some movement in the scene, like walking to see the bears. Player 4 should probably decide to be either an animal or a zookeeper given that the family are already established. Actors should feel free to change characters in the scene, provided it always makes sense and the story keeps evolving. Keep it moving, not just focused on ABCs for the most enjoyment! The scene should end when the last sentence begins with Z is spoken (not too hard with a 'Zoo' theme!)

2. Animal Characters

What: Basic scenes but with animal characteristics – fun! IMPROVISATION, CHARACTERIZATION

Techniques: VOICE, BODY, MOVEMENT, SPACE

How: Three to four Players for a scene. The audience chooses animals for each Player and a scene starter or topic. The players are not meant to 'become' the animals they have been given, but only to display certain traits the animal has. For instance, if one of the Players has been told they're a dog, they will act like a person for most of the scene, but at some point might try to nonchalantly "sniff the butt" of another player. In other words, the traits should be acted subtly rather than obviously (like barking). The scene should otherwise be normal.

3. Charades

What: Everyone should remember classic Charades, but if you don't, it's miming out people, places and things for others to guess. THINKING, LISTENING.

Techniques: BODY, MOVEMENT, SPACE

How: For the younger kids, I usually have photos of animals or objects on a card and show it to them privately. They will then mime the animal or object and the audience has to guess what they are. For older ones, I will have a range of animals, situations, movies, songs, and so on – all age appropriate, for them to mime out.

4. Counting Game

What: A basic scene game with a restricted number of words per player per sentence. IMPROVISATION, FOCUS, ACTION

Techniques: VOICE, BODY, MOVEMENT, SPACE

How: Three to four Players are on stage waiting to play a scene. Someone from the audience gives each of the Players a number between one and ten. Another audience member gives a scene starter or topic. Each of the players is only allowed to speak the exact number of words in a sentence as the number they have been given.

For example, in a scene about a "Band Rehearsal" Player 1, who has been given the number 3 starts by saying, "Come on guys!" While Player 2, who has been given the number 1, simply says, "What?" Player 3, who has been given the number 6 says, "He means come on let's practice", Player 2 says, "Oh." Player 1 says, "I'll start then." And so on. Be sure to encourage action and not just counting.

5. Directions

What: A fun moving and action game with a twist! LISTENING, ACTION

Techniques: BODY, MOVEMENT, SPACE, VOICE

How: This is a game to see how well the Players can follow directions. There are several different versions of this game, feel free to make up your own and add more directions as desired. Background music makes this more fun.

Players find a space in the room. The teacher or leader gives them the following directions at different times during the game:

- **Clap** – Players stop moving and clap their hands.
- **Jump** – Players stop moving and jump in the air.
- **Swizzle** - Players stop and turn around in a circle.
- **Twizzle** - Players stop and put their hands on their knees.
- **Go** - Players move around the space.
- **Stop** - Players stop and freeze.

It sounds easy, and it is! UNTIL, you throw in the twist! After the Players have gotten used to the Directions. Tell them to stop, freeze and listen, because you are going to turn the game inside out. Now, **Clap** will mean **Jump**, **Jump** will mean **Clap**, **Twizzle** and **Swizzle** are switched up too…so are **Stop** and **Go** – **Go** will mean to stop moving and **Stop** will mean to go.

You can play for 'Outs', where anyone doing the wrong movement is out – or you can just play for fun!

6. Expert Double Figure

What: Player A has no arms. Player B is Player A's arms...crazy strangeness! TEAMWORK, IMPROVISATION, SYNCHRONIZATION, TRUST

Techniques: BODY, MOVEMENT, SPACE, VOICE

How: This is a really funny game to watch and a class favorite, as long as the Players stick to rules of Safety and Respect. Trusting each other is very important and should be discussed before attempting this game.

Four Players are on stage either sitting or standing. Players A and C have their hands behind their backs while Players B and D stand or sit behind them playing A and C's arms by poking their arms through the armpits of A and C. The audience chooses what Player A (and arms B) are experts at, While Players C and D act as the Host or Interviewer of the "Expert". For example, Players A, with Arms B, is an expert at drawing horses. Therefore, Player C, with arms D, is supplied with a piece of paper and a pen to give to Player A (and Arms B) to demonstrate his or her expert horse drawing skills. Player A may then offer Player C a chance to have a try with Player A's expert instructions.

7. Emotional Boundaries

What: Scenes can change when the emotion behind them changes, but the rapid emotional changes in this game are hilarious. EMOTION, IMPROVISATION, TEAMWORK

Techniques: VOICE, BODY, MOVEMENT, SPACE

How: The stage is divided into three different "emotion zones". Three or four Players move about the stage, playing their scene but must take on the emotion of the zone they're in.

To use a simple example of "The Three Little Pigs", they might start out with each one being in their own "emotion zone": Little Pig 1 in 'Angry'; Little Pig 2 in 'Sad'; Little Pig 3 in 'Happy'. The zones stay the same as the scene changes. So, Little Pig 1 might be rightly 'Angry' when the Wolf comes knocking at the door (If there's a Player 4 playing the Wolf, he has to be angry in this zone too). However, when Little Pig 1's house is blown down and he runs to Little Pig 2's house, they are now in the 'Sad' zone and can no longer act angry. Neither can the Wolf, who is also suddenly sad when he enters this zone and blows down Little Pigs 2's house. The funny part will be trying to justify how everyone is suddenly happy with they are all at Little Pig 3's house!

8. Freeze

What: A scene is started the frozen. A Player takes over the exact position of another Player and starts a whole new scene. Improv at its finest!
IMPROVISATION, THINKING, TEAMWORK.

Technique: VOICE, BODY, MOVEMENT, SPACE

How: A scene starts with two or three players based on an audience member's suggestion. A Caller calls out "Freeze" at some point in the scene and another Player switches with a Player in the scene, taking on his or her EXACT position. Then the Caller yells "Unfreeze!" and an entirely new scene begins. This carries on until every Player has had a chance on stage.

9. Mister Hit

What: A fun ice breaking and name learning game with lots of movement!
ICE BREAKER, NAME LEARNING, ACTION, LISTENING, MEMORY

Techniques: VOICE, BODY, MOVEMENT, SPACE

How: If a group is just getting to know each other, you can start this game in a circle with everyone saying their names loud and clear. Next everyone mills around the space. One person is Mister Hit and put their hand up in the air so everyone can see who Mister Hit is, then says, "I'm Mister Hit, One, Two, Three!" Mister Hit then put one arm out in front in a grabbing position and chooses one person to walk towards – This is a walking game, not a running one, so be sure to emphasize safety and "walking only" at all times. As Mister Hit approaches his or her Target, the Target must call out another Players name before they are touched (not Hit) by Mister Hit. As soon as the other Player's name is called, THAT Player now becomes Mister Hit and must put their arm in the air and say, "I'm Mister Hit, One, Two, Three!" If a person is tagged, they are out. If you don't want to play with Outs you can play double ups, where the tagged Player becomes a second, third and fourth Mister Hit.

The game can get very fast and furious, so again, be safety conscious.

10. The Party Game

What: A bunch of wacky characters go to a party and the host has to guess who in the heck they are. CHARACTERIZATION, IMPROVISATION, LISTENING, TEAMWORK.

Techniques: VOICE, BODY, MOVEMENT, SPACE

How: One Player is choses to be the Party Host and must leave the room so that they cannot hear who their party guests will be. The audience chooses characters for the other Players – I suggest no more than four Party Guests as it can become too chaotic.

Once the Party Guests know who they are going to be, they must decide how to portray their character through their use of Voice, Body, Movement and Space techniques and without actually telling the Party Host who they are.

The Party Host sets up their party and the guests arrive one at a time. The Party Host must discover who his or her guests are by interacting with them and asking them questions.

When the Party Host has guessed who a character is, they must send them off stage in a creative way. For instance, if the Party Host has guessed that one of her guests is Sponge Bob Square Pants, she might say, "Hey Sponge Bob, thanks so much for coming to my party but I think Mr. Crabs was needing you to work today at the Crusty Crab! You'd better go or you'll be late!"

11. Sit, Stand, Kneel Lie Down

What: This is a game that explores the use of Space in Drama – no Player can occupy the same position on the stage at the same time.
IMPROVISATION, LEVELS, LISTENING.

Techniques: SPACE, BODY, MOVEMENT, VOICE

How: This is as much a listening game as it is a Levels game. Four Players are on the stage,, and each must take a different position: Lying down, sitting, standing and kneeling. Any Player can take on any of the four positions, but no Players are to take on the same position at any one time.

To add a layer of difficulty and interest, Players must ALWAYS justify the positions they have taken. For instance, if Player 1 is lying down, and suddenly Player 2 looks as if she is going to faint, just as Player 2 hits the ground in a lying down position, Player 1 might jump to a standing position because he had a cramp, or saw a spider! This might cause Player 3, who was already standing, to have to take on Player 2's original position, which was sitting…Player 3 has to justify sitting by saying or doing something like, "Gosh my feet are killing me!

12. Slow Motion Occupation

What: A game about taking a particular task and slowing it down, speeding it up, or reversing it. CHARACTERIZATION, TIME, ENERGY, MIME

Techniques: BODY, MOVEMENT, SPACE

How: Have students write down different occupations on scraps of paper and put them all into a hat. Everyone then starts milling around the room while the caller pulls an occupation out of a hat. Each person begins to mime a scene from this occupation. For instance, a "baker" might be kneading bread. Once everyone has their scene established, the caller calls out a "speed" – as in slow motion, fast forward, reverse, pause and play. Different occupations and speeds are called out during the game, which can increase in speed itself once the students are a bit more advanced.

13. Slow Motion Races/Olympics

What: A commentator leads the audience through a silly slow motion race or Olympic event. IMPROVISATION, PHYSICAL THEATRE, LISTENING, ACTION

Techniques: BODY, MOVEMENT, SPACE, VOICE

How: Three or four Players are on the stage. A Sports Commentator is on the side of the stage commenting on the proceedings. The audience can decide what event or type of race the Players are about to have. For instance, if it is the Nose Hair Pulling Olympics, then each of the Players can be "Warming-up" in very slow motion, getting ready to pull out the most nose hairs.

The goal is to exaggerate whatever it is that the Players are meant to be doing in very slow motion and to interact with each other so that the audience sees that they are actually in competition with each other.

There are so many ways to explore this game, but the goal should always be on over-exaggerating facial and body movements in super slow motion.

14. Soundscape

What: This is about audience participation and creating layers to a scene by adding a soundscape. SOUND, IMPROVISATION, TEAMWORK, TIMING, ACCEPTING OFFERS

Techniques: VOICE, BODY, MOVEMENT, SPACE

How: A basic scene is played by three to four Players, while the audience adds sound effects. We might hear footsteps when someone is walking across the stage, a dripping tap that one of the Players might need to look in to, or crickets in the night. The key is to not let the soundscape take over the scene, but to add to it. Players on stage must react to sounds as though they are truly part of the scene. For instance, if there is a car honking, the Players should not ignore it but either jump out of the way, or say something that acknowledges the reason for the honking.

15. Space Jump!

What: This is probably the most requested Drama game of all time. Scene change game. IMPROVISATION, TEAMWORK, ACCEPTING OFFERS

Techniques: VOICE, BODY, MOVEMENT, SPACE

How: I usually play this by dividing the class in half and calling the Team 1 and Team 2. Team 1 starts and Team 2 is the audience. The first Player on team 1 steps on to the stage and asks "Does anyone have a scene suggestion?" She should take the first appropriate suggestion she receives. She will then start the scene. Use of all the Drama techniques are encouraged. The Caller, who is usually the teacher yells, "Space Jump!" at some point in the scene and the Player freezes. Player 2 enters and starts an entirely new scene. "Space Jump!" is called again at some point in the next scene and so on until all of Team 1's Players are on stage. The scenes now go in reverse.

When the last member of the team is on stage the Caller yells "Space Jump!" and the last member goes off stage, and the scene continues as it had before the last "Space Jump!" and so on until it is left with the original beginning Player, who must then find a way to finish her scene.

16. Superhero Eulogy

What: A scene game where Players take turns filling in the blanks of the life story of the Superhero who has passed on. IMPROVISATION, ACCEPTING OFFERS, THINKING.

Techniques: VOICE, BODY, MOVEMENT, SPACE

How: Players are gathered around a made-up Superhero who has recently passed away. They are sad, and are each paying their respects. Some people in the game knew the superhero when they were a kid, another is his/her arch enemy. Someone else could talk about how the superhero met her fate (for example, simply tripping over her own shoelace and landing in quick drying cement face down). This should be done in a way that is funny rather than truly sad, otherwise the audience will be left feeling down.

17. Typewriter Scene

What: This was also a class favorite. One person is the 'storyteller' or 'writer' and the other Players act out the story as it is being written. CHARACTERIZATION, ACCEPTING OFFERS, IMPROVISATION, LISTENING.

Techniques: VOICE, BODY, MOVEMENT, SPACE

How: One Player, the 'Writer' types out a story and as he or she does so, the other Players come to life as characters in the story. The 'Writer' has most of the control as to how the story develops and the other Players should pay close attention so they can bring the story to life as the Writer wishes it to be.

For example, the Writer is writing (telling) a story about three horrible sisters (Three Players step forward and take on horrible characteristics – they may bicker between each other when the Writer pauses for their dialogue), who plot to kidnap a local beauty to make her their house slave (A Player steps forward to become 'The Local Beauty'). The Writer can either give the Players dialogue to say, or pause and allow the dialogue to come directly from the characters. The Writer should focus on a beginning, a middle and an end and not let the story go on too long.

18. Where Are We?

What: Players create an environment one at a time by choosing a pose and freezing, and the audience has to guess where the environment is. THINKING, LISTENING, TEAMWORK, IMPROVISATION

Techniques: VOICE, BODY, MOVEMENT, SPACE

How: Players draw an environment suggestion from a hat. They have 30 seconds to enter into the environment one at a time, pose, then freeze. At the end of the 30 seconds the audience must guess where and what the environment is.

For example, the Players choose "The Beach on a windy day". The first Player might jump in and strike a pose like she's getting sand blown in her face. The second Player might decide to be The Wind himself and grandly blow towards the first Player's direction. The third Player might become a beach towel that has wrapped itself around Player 1's legs, and so on. You can change the timing of course and make this a moving environment rather than a static one.

Exercises

1. **Elevator**

What: A fun and fantastic character exercise. CHARACTERIZATION, IMPROVISATION, ACCEPTING OFFERS

Techniques: BODY, MOVEMENT, SPACE – SOMETIMES VOICE

How: Usually this scene is played silent, but occasionally I have allowed dialogue. Characters get on an elevator at different floors, each displaying strong characteristics. The characters should complement each other in a way that advances and expands the scene.

For instance, if a character gets on the elevator as a frail old woman, the next character could be a helpful young boy who assists her when she drops her purse. Or, an annoying teenager could get on the elevator on one floor and her mother could get on on the next floor and scold her for shopping when she should be in school. Each character should ride the elevator for a couple of floors, get off and then get back on at some point, as a completely different character.

2. **Flocking**

What: This is a physical warm-up and ICE BREAKER. Think of Follow the Leader but in the shape of a pyramid...like a flock of birds. SYNCHRONIZATION

Techniques: MOVEMENT, BODY, SPACE

How: Groups of no less than 3, or as large as the whole class. Pyramid shape. One person in front, two behind them, three behind them and so on. Music or drum beats are great for this. The first person does a movement or dance move for eight counts while all others follow. Then everyone turns to the right, and the person to the right of the first person becomes the new leader and does their movement or dance move for eight counts and so on until everyone has had a chance to lead.

3. Group Stop

What: This is about moving, listening and focusing on each other.
LISTENING, FOCUS, SYNCHRONIZATION, TEAMWORK

Techniques: BODY, MOVEMENT

How: Everyone quietly starts moving around the space. One person (usually the teacher to start) will then freeze in position unexpectedly. As soon as the others notice a person has frozen, they also freeze. The goal is for everyone to freeze almost immediately after the first person freezes. Once everyone is frozen, it starts again. Anyone can be the initial freezer or the first person can secretly wink at the person who will be the next freezer.

4. Hello

What: This is an excellent exercise for demonstrating RELATIONSHIPS, STATUS and CHARACTER. It also works great as an ICE BREAKER.

Techniques: SPACE, BODY, MOVEMENT, VOICE

How: Players form two lines and face each other. If there are an uneven amount of Players, the host or teacher may step in so that everyone has a partner. Players should be about ten feet apart from each other if possible.

Players are going to walk towards each other several times, each with a different relationship to the person across from them in mind. The first time they walk towards each other, they should act as though they've never met. When they reach the opposite side, they face each other and the teacher will call out a different relationship: Casual friends, long-lost friends, BFFs, enemies, Boss and employee who was supposed to be home sick, King/Queen and servant, spies, police and criminal, Parent and child caught doing something naughty.

Be sure to emphasize that there should be no physical contact besides handshakes and hugs – this is mainly for the status relationships as I've had classes where some kids playing the parents went straight to smacking the "naughty kids". Safety should always be at the forefront, as sometimes lines can be blurred for younger actors.

5. Help Desk

What: Another fun character exercise where Players take turns asking for help from a very helpful Customer Service Agent. CHARACTERIZATION, ACCEPTING OFFERS, IMPROVISATION, LISTENING

Techniques: VOICE, BODY, MOVEMENT, SPACE

How: A Customer Service Agent sits or stands behind a counter or desk. This person is to be neutral and helpful at all times. In other words, their sole job is to make the customer happy. Customers are to approach the Agent one at a time, in strong character, and ask for a particular item or for some problem to be solved.

For example, an elderly man with no teeth and poor eyesight can't find the peanut butter. The Customer Service Agent is there to help!

6. Machines

What: Players must create an imaginary machine, complete with noises and movement. IMPROVISATION, TEAMWORK, TRUST

Techniques: BODY, MOVEMENT, SPACE, VOICE

How: Players enter one at a time and offer a repetitive movement and an accompanying noise. They should connect to one another somehow rather than just standing randomly around the stage – the goal is to create an imaginary machine. Players should make strong choices but avoid anything that they won't be able to sustain until all the Players join the piece (knee bends, push-ups). At the end, they can name the machine and say what it is used for.

7. Many Ways to Open a Door

What: Players must imagine that there is an unusual door on stage and behind that door is...well, it's up to the Player to decide! THINKING, IMAGINATION, PHYSICAL THEATER

Techniques: BODY, MOVEMENT, SPACE

How: Players move across the stage one at a time. They must open a door that they have imagined and once through the door, they must mime what they have found. The audience then gets a chance to guess what type of door they have opened what was on the other side.

For example, a Player discovers a miniature wooden door that is locked and then searches for the key. They find the key on a tiny table, open the door with it but of course they are too big to fit through. They then find a small cake on the table that wasn't there before. The cake has the words "Eat Me" written on it in icing....sound familiar? The trick is that this is all done in mime, so no talking.

8. Mirrors

What: A focus and physical listening exercise that explores movement, gesture and space. FOCUS, TEAMWORK, LISTENING

Techniques: SPACE, MOVEMENT, BODY

How: In pairs, Players take turns leading as though moving in a mirror. Players should move slowly enough so that they aren't trying to trick the other Player. The partners should frequently take turns leading and getting into a mirroring rhythm so that if someone were to watch them, they wouldn't know who was leading and who was following.

This exercise can be done sitting still or moving about the space.

9. Photograph

What: I call this Deconstructing a Photograph – it's a fun thinking exercise that encourages teamwork. TEAMWORK, THINKING, IMPROVISATION, ACTION, CHARACTERIZATION

Techniques: SPACE, BODY, MOVEMENT

How: You can have as many Players as you like join in this one but it must be one at a time. One Player steps into a scene, strikes a pose and freezes as though they're in a photograph. The next Player joins the scene and so on and so on. Each Player should think about how they can contribute to an overall scene that will eventually become the final photo.

The goal is for all the Players to work together to create a coherent, meaningful photograph, rather than a lot of individual, random people doing their own thing.

10. Video Tape Machine

What: A very simple scene that can be played forward, backward, paused and in Slo Mo thanks to a host with a remote control. IMPROVISATION, ACTION, LISTENING, THINKING.

Techniques: BODY, MOVEMENT, SPACE, VOICE

How: Kids might not even know what a VCR is, but they will understand the concept of Fast-forward, Rewind, Pause and Slow Motion – you can even add 'Next Scene' to the mix.

Players are acting out a basic scene, the simpler, the better. The host, or the teacher has a remote control that can stop the scene, pause it, reverse it, make it go into fast-forward mode, and so on.

11. Walking Like...

What: A sensory and character exercise. CHARACTERIZATION, SENSES, ACTION.

Techniques: BODY, MOVEMENT, SPACE

How: Players are milling around the room. You may have background music for this if you like. The teacher or leader call out different characters and situations and the Players have to "walk like..." they are that character or in that situation. Note: Although the title of this exercise is called "Walking Like..." anyone can participate whether they can walk or not. If they cannot walk, just have them imagine the character or situation where they are and how they are.

You might call out the following examples:

- A Giant
- A mouse
- You are in a snowstorm
- You are a very old man or woman
- You are walking through jello
- You have just stepped in something disgusting
- You are walking through mud
- You are walking on the moon
- You are an elephant
- You are a leaf blowing in the wind

12. Yes, And

What: A fun ACCEPTING OFFERS exercise!

Techniques: VOICE, BODY, MOVEMENT, SPACE

How: Two Players on the stage. One says a simple sentence (not a question) to the other like, "Great game today!" The Players must now always respond to each other starting with the words "Yes and..." So the other Player might say, "Yes and it's going to be an even greater game tomorrow!" Whereby the first Player might respond by saying, "Yes, and I heard the weather tomorrow will be excellent for the game!"

The goal is to expand the scene while supporting each other's responses.

Thanks for buying and reading my book!

I'm always happy to receive feedback and questions.

I also do Drama Coaching, so if you are in need of assistance, please feel free to get in touch!

You can find me at www.shaunarayratapu.com

Email: shauna@shaunarayratapu.com

SHAUNA RAY RATAPU AND STUDENT SOPHIE

Index

Accent, 37

Body, 35, 37, 38, 72, 86, 88, 89, 90, 91, 92, 93, 94, 95, 96, 98, 99, 100, 101, 102, 103, 104, 105, 106, 107, 108, 109, 110, 111, 112, 113, 114, 115, 116, 117, 118
budget, 55, 56, 63, 64

Capital Playhouse, **7**, **8**, **13**, **17**, **21**
Circle time, 33, 34
costume, 55, 61, 62

Direction, 39
Dress Rehearsal, 64, 65

Energy, 39
Ensemble Awareness, 39
Exercise, 34
Exercises
   Elevator, 76, 113
   Flocking, 75, 113
   Group Stop, 114
   Hello, 69, 114
   Help Desk, 71, 115
   Machines, 115
   Many Ways to Open a Door, *69*, 78, 116
   Mirrors, 116
   Photograph, 117
   Soundscape, 85
   Video Tape Machine, 117
   Walking Like…, 72, 81, 117, 118

Yes, And, 118
Eye contact, 38

Facial expression, 38

Games, 33
   Alphabet Game, 103
   Animal Characters, 103
   Charades, 78, 104
   Counting Game, 104
   Directions, 73, 75, 105
   Emotional Boundaries, 106
   Expert Double Figure, 105
   Freeze, 107
   Help Desk, 84
   Machines, 83
   Mister Hit, 82, 107, 108
   Mr. Hit, 71
   Sit, Stand, Kneel Lie Down, 109
   Slow Motion Occupation, 109
   Slow Motion Races/Olympics, 76, 78, 110
   Soundscape, 110
   Space Jump, 111
   Space Jump!, 68, 74, 76, 81, 86, 111
   Superhero Eulogy, 111
   The Party Game, 85, 86, 108
   Typewriter Scene, 112
   Where are we?, 83, 112
General space, 41
Group Movement, 39

Imagination, 17, 116

Improvisation, 17, 90, 91, 93, 95, 98, 101, 103, 104, 106, 107, 108, 109, 110, 111, 112, 113, 115, 117
inclusion, 16

Lesson, 33, 48
Levels, 41
lighting, 22, 42, 55, 57, 60, 63, 64

Mime, 78, 80, 109
Movement, 17, 35, 37, 38, 39, 86, 88, 89, 90, 91, 92, 93, 94, 95, 96, 98, 101, 102, 103, 104, 105, 106, 107, 108, 109, 110, 111, 112, 113, 114, 115, 116, 117, 118

Once on This Island, 7

Pace, 36
Pathways, 39
Pause, 36, 117
Personal space, 41
Pitch, 36
Policy and Procedure, 43
Posture, 38
Props, 62
Proximity, 42

Repetition, 39
resources, 55, 56, 57, 59
Role-Playing, 17

SAFETY, 31, 32
Schedule, 56
SET, 63
Shooting Starz Creative Drama Workshops, 9

sound, 55, 57, 59, 60, 64, 93, 94, 95, 99, 100, 101, 102, 110, 116
Space, 21, 35, 37, 39, 40, 41, 69, 78, 86, 88, 89, 90, 91, 92, 93, 94, 95, 96, 98, 101, 102, 103, 104, 105, 106, 107, 108, 109, 110, 111, 112, 113, 114, 115, 116, 117, 118
stage, 23, 36, 38, 42, 45, 55, 63, 88, 103, 104, 106, 109, 115, 116
Story-telling, 17

Teamwork, 92, 93, 103, 106, 107, 108, 110, 111, 112, 114, 115, 116, 117
The Actor's Tools, 86
Timing, 39
Tone, 36

Unhinged Productions, 10

Voice, 17, 35, 36, 37, 72, 84, 86, 88, 89, 90, 91, 92, 93, 94, 95, 96, 98, 99, 100, 101, 102, 103, 104, 105, 106, 107, 108, 109, 110, 111, 112, 113, 114, 115, 117, 118
Voice Projection, 17
Volume, 36

Warm ups, 33, 88
1 to 20, 88
Alien, Tiger, Cow, 88
Bippity Bippity Bop, 82, 89
Circle Dance, 80, 90
Dude!, 90
Everyone Who, 91
Free Association, 91
Group juggle, 74, 92
HA!, 78, 92

Hands, 93
Hello, 97, 114
Jam Session, 93
Name Ball, 70, 94
Name Game, 94
Pass Catch, 95
Ping Pong Poo, 95
Pinocchio, 72, 95

Popcorn, 86, 97
Song Circle, 98
Stretching, 98
The Name Game, 68
Voice Warm-Up, 99
What are you doing?, 70, 72, 78, 84, 101, 102
Yes, Let's!, 80, 102

Printed in Great Britain
by Amazon